New Directions for
Institutional Research

John F. Ryan
EDITOR-IN-CHIEF

Gloria Crisp
ASSOCIATE EDITOR

D1594298

Measuring Glass Ceiling Effects in Higher Education: Opportunities and Challenges

Jerlando F. L. Jackson
Elizabeth M. O'Callaghan
Raul A. Leon

EDITORS

Number 159
Jossey-Bass
San Francisco

MEASURING GLASS CEILING EFFECTS IN HIGHER EDUCATION: OPPORTUNITIES AND CHALLENGES
Jerlando F. L. Jackson, Elizabeth M. O'Callaghan, Raul A. Leon (eds.)
New Directions for Institutional Research, no. 159
John F. Ryan, Editor-in-Chief
Gloria Crisp, Associate Editor

NEW DIRECTIONS FOR INSTITUTIONAL RESEARCH (ISSN 0271-0579, electronic ISSN 1536-075X) is part of The Jossey-Bass Higher and Adult Education Series and is published quarterly by Wiley Subscription Services, Inc., A Wiley Company, at Jossey-Bass, One Montgomery Street, Suite 1200, San Francisco, California 94104-4594 (publication number USPS 098-830). POSTMASTER: Send address changes to New Directions for Institutional Research, Jossey-Bass, One Montgomery Street, Suite 1200, San Francisco, California 94104-4594.

INDIVIDUAL SUBSCRIPTION RATE (in USD): $89 per year US/Can/Mex, $113 rest of world; institutional subscription rate: $317 US, $357 Can/Mex, $391 rest of world. Single copy rate: $29. Electronic only–all regions: $89 individual, $317 institutional; Print & Electronic–US: $98 individual, $365 institutional; Print & Electronic–Canada/Mexico: $98 individual, $405 institutional; Print & Electronic–Rest of World: $122 individual, $439 institutional.

EDITORIAL CORRESPONDENCE should be sent to John F. Ryan at jfryan@uvm.edu.

New Directions for Institutional Research is indexed in *Academic Search* (EBSCO), *Academic Search Elite* (EBSCO), *Academic Search Premier* (EBSCO), *CIJE: Current Index to Journals in Education* (ERIC), *Contents Pages in Education* (T&F), EBSCO Professional Development Collection (EBSCO), *Educational Research Abstracts Online* (T&F), ERIC Database (Education Resources Information Center), *Higher Education Abstracts* (Claremont Graduate University), *Multicultural Education Abstracts* (T&F), *Sociology of Education Abstracts* (T&F).

Microfilm copies of issues and chapters are available in 16mm and 35mm, as well as microfiche in 105mm, through University Microfilms, Inc., 300 North Zeeb Road, Ann Arbor, Michigan 48106-1346.

www.josseybass.com

THE ASSOCIATION FOR INSTITUTIONAL RESEARCH (AIR) is the world's largest professional association for institutional researchers. The organization provides educational resources, best practices, and professional development opportunities for more than 4,000 members. Its primary purpose is to support members in the process of collecting, analyzing, and converting data into information that supports decision making in higher education.

CONTENTS

EDITORS' NOTES

An analysis of the U.S. workforce shows that women and people of color represent an increasing share of employment in the economy in areas previously dominated by White men such as the corporate sector (Winborne, 2007). According to the Hudson Institute, women now account for almost half of the total workforce (47%), and it is predicted that representation for people of color will surpass the 30% mark by 2020 (California Diversity Council, 2005). Despite this increased presence in the workforce, we still know very little in regard to why these two groups continue to be underrepresented in senior-level positions. The lack of empirical and practice-based examinations of glass ceiling effects helps ensure that this unique form of discrimination remains an often-misunderstood topic (Jackson & Leon, 2010; Moore, 1995).

Purpose of This Volume

The purpose of this volume is to provide a comprehensive resource to enhance our understanding of glass ceiling effects in higher education. Within this text, particular emphasis is placed on establishing the rationale for examining the nature of glass ceiling effects as a phenomenon that continues to negatively impact women and people of color in the workforce. The volume is organized to guide the reader across seven chapters that approach the glass ceiling from a myriad of perspectives and offer compelling arguments concerning the need for additional research on this topic. These chapters highlight the need for data collection for institutional planning purposes, not only to advise key decision makers but also to better understand how the glass ceiling impacts women and people of color in higher education.

At the core of this volume is the premise that gathering institutional data on the glass ceiling for planning purposes should be a priority to inform institutional leaders on workforce composition matters. Drawing on the current literature on glass ceiling effects in the higher education workforce, this volume provides a heuristic foundation to basic concepts that define this phenomenon in institutions of higher education. A key feature of the volume is its inclusion of examples illustrating how data on glass ceiling effects can be collected, analyzed, and applied to make informed decisions regarding policy and practice in colleges and universities.

Chapters in this volume provide institutional decision makers with valuable information to confront the challenge of glass ceiling effects and provide a much needed context for examining how they manifest across different institutional environments. Responding to a gap in the literature, this volume demonstrates the applicability of glass ceiling effects research

New Directions for Institutional Research, no. 159 © 2014 Wiley Periodicals, Inc.
Published online in Wiley Online Library (wileyonlinelibrary.com) • DOI: 10.1002/ir.20049

for institutional researchers, providing not only step-by-step protocols to collect and analyze glass ceiling data but also rich examples across different institutional contexts. The chapters that follow focus specifically on the potential of qualitative research to examine questions centered on employment disparities and glass ceiling effects; others scrutinize this phenomenon in the context of historically Black colleges and universities or provide an overview and assessment of computer software designed specifically to assist institutions in exploring glass ceiling effects. Still others discuss the implications of moving from theory into practice, offering a systematic overview of glass ceiling effects in higher education.

Establishing the Historical Problem of the Glass Ceiling

The term glass ceiling itself was originally coined in the *Wall Street Journal* in 1986 (Hymowitz & Schellhardt, 1986), and it is used to describe "a barrier so subtle that it is transparent, yet so strong that it prevents women and minorities from moving up in the management hierarchy" (Morrison & Von Glinow, 1990, p. 200). Since the 1980s, a large body of research emerging from various employment sectors of the economy has documented this phenomenon. But, for the most part, the concept of glass ceiling effects as a measure of inequity has been studied largely within the business and public administration literature, where it has been broadly defined as a set of "artificial barriers based on attitudinal organizational bias that prevent qualified individuals from advancing upward in their organization into management-level positions" (Martin, 1991, p. 1).

The Federal Government began dedicating resources to address the glass ceiling phenomenon in the U.S. workforce in the early 1990s (Martin, 1991, 1992). More specifically, the U.S. Department of Labor introduced its glass ceiling initiative in 1991, which set the foundation for the creation of the Glass Ceiling Commission, which explored the workforce composition in the United States' business sector (Federal Glass Ceiling Commission, 1995b). The Federal Glass Ceiling Commission gathered information at the management level in the private sector on historically underrepresented groups including: women, African Americans/Blacks, American Indians, Asians/Pacific Islanders, and Hispanics. These data gathered by the Federal Glass Ceiling Commission revealed that these groups have made considerable strides gaining representation in the workforce for the past four decades since the introduction of Title VII of the 1964 Civil Rights Act—a milestone that outlawed employment discrimination practices on the basis of race, color, religion, sex, and national origin (Kochan et al., 2003). The commission also revealed that there remains considerable work to be done removing persistent barriers that hinder access for these groups to senior-level positions (Federal Glass Ceiling Commission, 1995a).

While these initial efforts were primarily concerned with remedying inequities in management positions within the corporate sector, the findings of the Glass Ceiling Commission brought national attention to the hiring practices that resulted in a more diverse workforce, and in turn, served as a clarion call for researchers to examine gender and race inequalities across other workforce sectors. In addition to the aforementioned research and others (Powell & Butterfield, 1994) sponsored by the U.S. Federal Government and the business sector (Morrison & Von Glinow, 1990; Morrison, White, Van Velsor, & the Center for Creative Leadership, 1987; Robinson & Dechant, 1997; Winborne, 2007), a growing body of literature has examined the roots of the glass ceiling as a unique form of discrimination within the armed forces (Baldwin, 1996a, 1996b) and within higher education (Chliwniak, 1997; David & Woodward, 1998; Johnsrud, 1991).

However, considering that almost 50 years have passed since the introduction of the Civil Rights Act in 1964, it is worrisome that the glass ceiling still stands as a major barrier for women and people of color. Its causes and its scope remain little understood, and specific research is needed that better measures glass ceiling effects in order to develop effective policies and recommendations to reduce and eradicate the phenomenon.

What Is the Definition of the Glass Ceiling?

In a comprehensive review of the glass ceiling literature, Jackson and O'Callaghan (2007) conclude that the phrase "glass ceiling" is an "imprecise and misunderstood term, used to describe a multiplicity of concepts" and employed more for its "shock" value than its explanatory utility (p. ii). Often it does not denote any particular kind of discrimination distinguishable from other forms of inequality. Across the literature, the glass ceiling is generally defined as the set of impediments and/or barriers to career advancement women and people of color encounter, increasing in severity with movement up the occupational hierarchy after controlling for productivity-relevant factors (Baxter & Wright, 2000; Cotter, Hermsen, Ovadia, & Vanneman, 2001; Maume, 2004; Morrison & Von Glinow, 1990).

These impediments and/or barriers span a constellation of variables that often manifest as conscious and subconscious discriminatory practices (Lee, 2002; Martin, 1991, 1992; Padavic & Reskin, 2002; Ridgeway, 2001). The glass ceiling manifests in multiple ways, and not only describes acrimonious experiences in the workplace but also more traditional forms of discrimination that emerge as part of the workplace social environment, job requirements, and cultural biases (Cotter et al., 2001). These forms of discrimination often include, although are not limited to, disparities in job position (e.g., rank, authority, and title), significant gaps in earnings, slower promotion rates, and lower levels of responsibility (as expressed through budgetary discretion and control; Ards, Brintnall, & Woodward, 1997; Athey, Avery, & Zemsky, 2000; Cotter, Hermsen, & Vanneman, 1999; Cotter et al., 2001; Ginther & Hayes, 1999; Landau, 1995).

NEW DIRECTIONS FOR INSTITUTIONAL RESEARCH • DOI: 10.1002/ir

Together these forms of discrimination create an artificial "ceiling" that limits employees' professional advancement within the organization. However, to provide a framework for the examination of the glass ceiling in the future that acknowledges a multitude of perspectives, it is important to utilize a definition that brings together all of what we know about the glass ceiling. Borrowing from the work of Cotter et al. (2001), we propose a broader definition that captures the full scope of what the concept entails.

Namely, a glass ceiling is a unique form of discrimination characterized by gender or racial inequalities that are not explained by other job-relevant characteristics of the employee. A glass ceiling occurs over a course of a career; it increases as one moves up the organizational hierarchy; and it is present if there is a difference in the chance of advancement of women and people of color to senior-level positions, and not purely in the representation of these groups at that level.

Glass Ceiling Effects in Higher Education

Issues such as workforce diversity, workplace discrimination, and employment disparities in higher education have been directly or indirectly studied over the past 20 years. Most of the previous research on the glass ceiling is focused on gender inequities (Bernhardt, Morris, & Handcock, 1995; Davies-Netzley, 1998), and very little of the scholarship about the glass ceiling is informed by research on race/ethnicity (Jackson & O'Callaghan, 2009).

As noted by Jackson and O'Callaghan (2009), the exploration of glass ceiling effects in higher education is a relatively young and growing area of research, and only a few studies differentiate or make a clear distinction between general inequities and glass ceiling effects in higher education (Johnsrud, 1991; Lee, 2002; Sagaria, 1988; Turner & Myers, 2000). Enhancing the body of literature and developing practical recommendations to address the glass ceiling has emerged as a growing area of concern, particularly given that higher education is one of the largest employment sectors in the U.S. economy. The environment of higher education has also been shown to be less receptive than other sectors of the economy to diverse groups, especially women and people of color (Bain & Cummings, 2000; Burbridge, 1994; Jackson & Leon, 2010). With over three million full-time and part-time employees nationwide (Jennifer, 2005), it is imperative to understand how the presence of a glass ceiling shapes the current workforce composition in higher education, determining what this phenomenon means for current work conditions and the future of higher education as an employment sector.

Existing data reveal the presence of a glass ceiling for women and people of color in the academy. These two groups in particular are underrepresented in senior-level positions, continue to receive lower salaries, are overrepresented in lower academic ranks, and often advance in the faculty track only in certain types of institutions such as two-year colleges and less prestigious four-year institutions (Chliwniak, 1997; Jackson & O'Callaghan, 2009; Jennifer, 2005; Trower & Chait, 2002). As a result, despite 30 years of affirmative action, the number of women and people of color in senior-level positions in higher education remains low (Jackson, 2004; Jackson & Daniels, 2007), and full-time faculty at highly regarded universities remain largely White and male (Trower & Chait, 2002).

With respect to the status of women in higher education, female graduate students were awarded 57% of master's degrees and 44% of doctoral degrees in the year 2000 (Trower & Chait, 2002). However, 84% of presidents, 83% of business officers, and 75% of academic deans are male (Corrigan, 2002). In addition, significant differences persist among faculty appointments. While women represent almost 40% of the full-time faculty positions in the country, only 24% of all full professors are women, and "the gap between percentage of tenured men and the percentage of tenured women has not changed in 30 years" (Trower & Chait, 2002, What's the Problem?, para. 4). Regarding salary inequities, on average, women earn $4,400 less than their male counterparts in two-year colleges, and $8,350 less in doctoral-granting institutions for faculty with a full professor status (Trower & Chait, 2002).

Statistics describing workforce composition and the status of people of color in higher education in 2001 indicate that faculty of color made up approximately 15% of all faculty in higher education. Moreover, fully 91% of full-time professors at research universities are White (Trower & Chait, 2002), while people of color continue to be employed largely in faculty positions below the assistant professor level (Trower & Chait, 2002). Likewise, very few people of color serve at the levels of executive, administrative, and managerial positions at prestigious institutions, where the glass ceiling is more pervasive and where Whites occupy the overwhelming majority (83%) of these positions (Harvey, 1999; Jennifer, 2005).

Prior research has emphasized that when examining the population of people of color, it is important to disaggregate data by race and ethnicity to understand how the glass ceiling impacts each subgroup. Ards et al. (1997) conclude that race/ethnicity is the most significant explanation for persistent differences in rank among faculty. The level of representation among African Americans in faculty positions is practically the same as in 1979, and they are less likely to obtain full professorship status or tenure when compared to White faculty (Bradburn, Sikora, & Zimbler, 2002). Likewise, 24% of all African Americans and 25% of all Hispanic full-time faculty are employed at the instructor and/or lecturer level, while only 17% of all White faculty hold these positions.

When positions of leadership are examined, the story is much the same. In a study of 3,896 university president posts in 2004, Whites were shown to hold 86.3% of these positions (Jennifer, 2005). While this number matches the total composition of faculty in the country in the aggregate (15% faculty of color; 85% White faculty), it is important to consider variation by institutional type since leadership roles are perceived and judged differently according to the type of institution (Jackson & O'Callaghan, 2009). For example, the concentration of people of color in president positions in two-year institutions is higher than the concentration of White presidents. More specifically, while 39% of all African American/Black presidents and 44% of all Hispanic presidents serve in two-year institutions, the number for White presidents at these institutions only reaches 36% (Jennifer, 2005). In contrast, 64% of White presidents hold this post at four-year institutions, compared to 60.9% of African Americans and 55.6% of all Hispanic presidents (Jennifer, 2005; Ryu, 2008). This disparity is put in sharper relief when examining private institutions, where 92% of all presidents are White (Ryu, 2008).

Furthermore, it is necessary to consider the impact of minority-serving institutions on the aggregate statistics since "virtually all of the HBCUs are headed by African-Americans and more than one-third of Hispanic-serving institutions [HSIs] are headed by Hispanics" (Jennifer, 2005, p. 20). As such, understanding what is occurring at the senior leadership level in higher education requires accounting for this portion of the overall numbers. It is also worth noting that while 5.2% of all faculty with full professor status in the country belong to the Asian/Pacific Islander group, only 0.9% have reached the rank of president—a relatively low figure considering that African Americans/Blacks held 5.8% of all presidencies, and Hispanics accounted for 4.6% in 2006 (Ryu, 2008).

Key Considerations and Challenges

One of the major challenges we confront is that glass ceiling effects have not generally been applied to studying employment disparities in the academic workforce; therefore, little is known about how to measure its presence, determine its impact on individuals and organizations, and generate strategies for countering a phenomenon hidden beneath layers of institutional culture (Jackson & Leon, 2010). The lack of prior research—in particular research that focuses on people of color—and data limitations, such as a lack of data disaggregated by race/ethnicity and gender, pose major barriers as we attempt to craft solutions to reduce or eliminate this phenomenon. Jackson and O'Callaghan (2009) contend that there is a unique intersecting relationship between gender and race with respect to glass ceiling effects, and until we understand this relationship, we will continue to disregard important features of the glass ceiling's real negative consequences. For example, a female faculty member who is also part of an underrepresented ethnic group may face potential barriers not only as a woman but also as part of a racial group that is underrepresented in the academy.

We must emphasize that individuals may often experience discrimination in more than one manner simultaneously, with different groups in different contexts in different ways (Maume, 2004). As Morley (2006a)

NEW DIRECTIONS FOR INSTITUTIONAL RESEARCH • DOI: 10.1002/ir

argued, there are a multitude of relationships that must be considered, and as long as we continue to ignore how gender intersects with identity characteristics such as race, ethnicity, disability, class, sexuality, and others, we will continue to fall short in understanding and addressing the breadth of glass ceiling effects.

Lastly, Jackson (2003) highlights how the lack of diversity in senior-level positions in institutions of higher education constitutes only the visible portion of a larger problem. When examining how the glass ceiling impacts workforce dynamics in higher education, individuals and organizations cannot ignore what hides beneath the surface, embedded in the core of each institution, where unwelcoming environments are nourished by practices of discrimination and the views of a dominant majority.

Effective interventions addressing glass ceiling effects require becoming aware of these embedded characteristics because when "power is relayed through seemingly trivial incidents and transactions" that include "sarcasm, jokes, exclusions, and throwaway remarks," it creates an environment propitious for the glass ceiling, and it becomes extremely difficult to disrupt these effects through the implementation of policies (Morley, 2006b, pp. 543–544). As Jackson (2003) posits, the underrepresentation of women and people of color at the top of the organizational hierarchy may only be the tip of the iceberg. The glass ceiling will continue to subtly deter these two groups from reaching senior-level positions in higher education until we dedicate time and effort to collect and analyze data that provide key institutional decision makers with valuable information to address this phenomenon.

Gathering Institutional Data for Planning Purposes

Most colleges and universities today collect racial and ethnic group information based on current U.S. Department of Education reporting classifications. These include: African American/Black (non-Hispanic), Asian American/Pacific Islander, Hispanic/Latino, American Indian/Alaskan Native, and White (not Hispanic or Latino). Institutional data factbooks also report other items such as gender composition of the workforce, salary, number of faculty at different ranks, and other variables that can play a key role when examining the workforce composition in higher education. Because institutions already collect these data, there is an opportunity for systematic analysis of glass ceiling effects, and institutional researchers should consider the best ways of harnessing these empirical tools to further scrutinize the realities of discrimination and inequalities across their own institutions. We recommend conducting glass ceiling research as part of the "standard" data analysis that institutions engage in to better build a knowledge base that will allow individuals and institutions to develop measures to confront this phenomenon.

Today, it is imperative that institutions of higher education continue to collect this type of data because the glass ceiling is a phenomenon that must be measured in a precise way. Of the growing body of research concerned with the examination of the glass ceiling, only a few studies have attempted to differentiate or make a clear distinction between general inequities and glass ceiling effects in higher education (Johnsrud, 1991; Lee, 2002; Sagaria, 1988; Turner & Myers, 2000), and even fewer have attempted to construct tools for rigorously measuring glass ceiling effects. One of the rare examples of such efforts, Cotter et al. (2001), proposes a four-prong empirical test to measure for the existence of a glass ceiling that has served as the skeleton for other studies (Maume, 2004) as well as our work in seeking to understand glass ceiling effects. The four prongs of the test are: first, a glass ceiling represents a gender or racial difference that is not explained by other job-relevant characteristics of the employee; second, a glass ceiling is also associated with greater disparities at higher levels of an outcome rather than lower levels; third, glass ceiling effects reside in the opportunities for advancement into higher levels, not merely in the proportion of individuals currently at those higher levels; and lastly, disparities in advancement and opportunity must increase over the course of a career.

Taking these four criteria into consideration, it becomes apparent that to adequately measure glass ceiling effects, longitudinal data sets are required that track the glass ceiling as a phenomenon over entire careers. Today, work has emerged measuring the first and second criteria that demonstrate the presence of glass ceiling effects in senior-level positions in the academic workforce. However, we argue that institutions of higher education can become key players in understanding this phenomenon, as they continue to build data sets that will allow researchers to measure the third and fourth criteria. For example, investigation into the third criterion, which focuses on opportunities for advancement, not merely the proportion of individuals currently at higher levels, requires the use of cohort data that are currently unavailable for higher education professionals in any existing national data set. Longitudinal studies are also necessary for testing the fourth criterion, which requires demonstrating how disparities in career advancement and opportunity increase over the course of a career.

Conclusion

This survey of the scholarly terrain demonstrates how much more investigation is needed to better understand the nature of glass ceiling effects in higher education. Considering the complexities of the phenomenon and its serious consequences, work in this area demands an intensive time commitment and often the cooperation and involvement of institutional researchers at colleges and universities who are in a position to help us understand how the glass ceiling impacts workforce dynamics in our society. There is an opportunity to fill a gap in the literature that will illustrate why the glass ceiling is not a simple form of discrimination, and why it is such a pervasive and concealed phenomenon with weighty implications for women and people of color and their future career aspirations.

As Phillips (2002) notes, workforce development issues tend to be top agenda items for most organizations, and this prioritization must also take hold in higher education. Careful inclusive planning must be attentive to intersecting identity characteristics presented by diverse individuals. Additionally, researchers must consider how these characteristics are displayed in various working and organizational contexts. To achieve these objectives, leaders in higher education must understand and address specific forms of workplace discrimination that have been documented across the literature (e.g., glass ceiling, disparate impact, and underutilization). These forms of discrimination may not always be present in isolation, or they may appear only in a secluded context. Therefore, comprehending their singular effects at the individual and organizational levels presents a challenge to researchers but one that must be grappled with in order to facilitate our quest for adequate responses to workforce diversity issues.

Acknowledgments

The editors are grateful to their support systems that provided them the space to complete this volume. Professionally, they are appreciative to their respective universities, academic departments, and colleagues. Personally, they are thankful for their families and friends allowing time for them to work on this project. The editors would like to acknowledge the extensive feedback and input provided by Benjamin Toff of Wisconsin's Equity and Inclusion Laboratory at the University of Wisconsin-Madison.

Dedication

Jerlando F. L. Jackson dedicates this volume to his Grandfather—Lucius Cushion. He passed away during the completion of this project. "Your name will live on through my published work."

Jerlando F. L. Jackson
Elizabeth M. O'Callaghan
Raul A. Leon
Editors

References

Ards, S., Brintnall, M., & Woodard, M. (1997). The road to tenure and beyond for African American political scientists. *The Journal of Negro Education, 66*, 159–171.

Athey, S., Avery, C., & Zemsky, P. (2000). Mentoring and diversity. *The American Economic Review, 90*, 765–786.

Bain, O., & Cummings, W. (2000). Academe's glass ceiling: Societal, professional, organizational, and institutional barriers to the career advancement of academic women. *Comparative Education Review, 44*(4), 493–514.

Baldwin, N. J. (1996a). Female promotions in male-dominant organizations: The case of the United States military. *The Journal of Politics, 58*(4), 1184–1197.

Baldwin, N. J. (1996b). The promotion record of the United States army: Glass ceilings in the officer corps. *Public Administration Review, 56*(2), 199–206.

Baxter, J., & Wright, E. O. (2000). The glass ceiling hypothesis: A comparative study of the United States, Sweden, and Australia. *Gender and Society, 14*(2), 275–294.

Bernhardt, A., Morris, M., & Handcock, M. S. (1995). Women's gains or men's losses? A closer look at the shrinking gender gap in earnings. *The American Journal of Sociology, 101*, 302–328.

Bradburn, E. M., Sikora, A. C., & Zimbler, L. J. (2002). *Gender and racial/ethnic differences in salary and other characteristics of postsecondary faculty: Fall 1988* (NCES 2002-170). Washington, DC: U.S. Department of Education.

Burbridge, L. C. (1994). *The glass ceiling in different sectors of the economy: Differences between government, non-profit, and for-profit organizations.* The Federal Glass Ceiling Commission, and Wellesley College Center for Research on Women. Wellesley, MA: Wellesley College, Center for Research on Women.

California Diversity Council. (2005). *Diversity: A business need.* Retrieved from http://californiadiversitycouncil.org/businessneed.html

Chliwniak, L. (1997). *Higher education leadership: Analyzing the gender gap* [ASHE-ERIC Higher Education Report, 25(4), 1–97]. Washington, DC: Graduate School of Education and Human Development, The George Washington University.

Corrigan, M. E. (2002). *The American college president.* Washington, DC: The American Council on Education Center for Policy Analysis.

Cotter, D. A., Hermsen, J. M., Ovadia, S., & Vanneman, R. (2001). The glass ceiling effect. *Social Forces, 80*, 655–681.

Cotter, D. A., Hermsen, J. M., & Vanneman, R. (1999). Systems of gender, race, and class inequality: Multilevel analyses. *Social Forces, 78*, 433–460.

David, M., & Woodward, D. (Eds.). (1998). *Negotiating the glass ceiling: Careers of senior women in the academic world.* London, UK: Falmer Press.

Davies-Netzley, S. A. (1998). Women above the glass ceiling: Perceptions on corporate mobility and strategies for success. *Gender and Society, 12*, 339–355.

Federal Glass Ceiling Commission. (1995a). *A solid investment: Making full use of the nation's human capital.* Washington, DC: U.S. Department of Labor.

Federal Glass Ceiling Commission. (1995b). *Good for business: Making full use of the nation's human capital: An environmental scan.* Washington, DC: U.S. Department of Labor.

Ginther, D. K., & Hayes, K. J. (1999). Gender differences in salary and promotion in the humanities. *The American Economic Review, 94*, 397–402.

Harvey, W. B. (Ed.). (1999). *Grass roots and glass ceilings: African American administrators in predominantly White colleges and universities.* Albany, NY: SUNY Press.

Hymowitz, C., & Schellhardt, T. (1986). The corporate woman: A special report. *The Wall Street Journal*, Section 4, 1D–24D.

Jackson, J. F. L. (2003). Toward administrative diversity: An analysis of the African American male educational pipeline. *The Journal of Men's Studies, 12*, 43–60.

Jackson, J. F. L. (2004). Engaging, retaining, and advancing African Americans to executive-level positions: A descriptive and trend analysis of academic administrators in higher and postsecondary education. *Journal of Negro Education, 73*(1), 4–20.

Jackson, J. F. L., & Daniels, B. D. (2007). A national progress report of African Americans in the administrative workforce in higher education. In J. F. L. Jackson (Ed.), *Strengthening the educational pipeline for African Americans: Informing research, policy, and practice* (pp. 115–137). Albany, NY: SUNY Press.

Jackson, J. F. L., & Leon, R. A. (2010). Enlarging our understanding of glass ceiling effects with social closure theory in higher education. In J. C. Smart (Ed.), *Higher education: Handbook of theory and research* (Vol. 25, pp. 351–379). London/New York: Springer.

Jackson, J. F. L., & O'Callaghan, E. M. (2007). *The glass ceiling: A misunderstood form of discrimination.* Milwaukee: Institute on Race and Ethnicity, University of Wisconsin System.

Jackson, J. F. L., & O'Callaghan, E. M. (2009). What do we know about the glass ceiling effect? A taxonomy and critical review to inform higher education research. *Research in Higher Education, 50*(5), 460–482.

Jennifer, F. G. (2005). *Minorities and women in higher education and the role of mentoring in their advancement.* Austin, TX: Office of Academic Affairs University of Texas System.

Johnsrud, L. K. (1991). Administrative promotion: The power of gender. *The Journal of Higher Education, 62*(2), 119–149.

Kochan, T., Bezrukova, K., Ely, R., Jackson, S., Joshi, A., Jehn, K., . . . Thomas, D. (2003). The effects of diversity on business performance: Report of the diversity research network. *Human Resource Management, 42*(1), 3–22.

Landau, J. (1995). The relationship of race and gender to managers' ratings of promotion potential. *Journal of Organizational Behavior, 16*, 391–400.

Lee, S. M. (2002). Do Asian American faculty face a glass ceiling? *American Educational Research Journal, 39*(3), 695–724.

Martin, L. (1991). *A report on the glass ceiling commission.* Washington, DC: U.S. Department of Labor.

Martin, L. (1992). *Pipelines of progress: A status report on the glass ceiling.* Washington, DC: U.S. Department of Labor.

Maume, D. J., Jr. (2004). Is the glass ceiling a unique form of inequality? Evidence from a random-effects model of managerial attainment. *Work and Occupations, 31*(2), 250–274.

Moore, D. D. (Ed.). (1995). *More letters from the American farmer: An edition of the essays in English left unpublished by Crévecoeur.* Athens, GA: University of Georgia Press.

Morley, L. (2006a). Including women: Gender in commonwealth higher education. *Women's Studies International Forum, 29*(6), 539–542.

Morley, L. (2006b). Hidden transcripts: The micropolitics of gender in commonwealth universities. *Women's Studies International Forum, 29*(6), 543–551.

Morrison, A. M., & Von Glinow, M. A. (1990). Women and minorities in management. *American Psychologist, 45*, 200–208.

Morrison, A. M., White, R. P., Van Velsor, E., & the Center for Creative Leadership. (1987). *Breaking the glass ceiling: Can women reach the top of America's largest corporations?* New York, NY: Addison-Wesley.

Padavic, I., & Reskin, B. (2002). *Women and men at work* (2nd ed.). Thousand Oaks, CA: Pine Forge Press.

Phillips, R. (2002). Recruiting and retaining a diverse faculty. *Planning for Higher Education, 30*, 30–39.

Powell, G. N., & Butterfield, D. A. (1994). Investigating the 'Glass Ceiling' phenomenon: An empirical study of actual promotions to top management. *Academy of Management Journal, 37*(1), 68–86.

Ridgeway, C. L. (2001). Gender, status and leadership. *Journal of Social Issues, 57*, 637–655.

Robinson, G., & Dechant, K. (1997). Building a business case for diversity. *The Academy of Management Executive, 2*, 21–31.

Ryu, M. (2008). *Minorities in higher education 2008: 23rd status report.* Washington, DC: American Council on Education.

Sagaria, M. M. (1988). Administrative mobility and gender. *Higher Education, 59*, 305–326.

Trower, C. A., & Chait, R. P. (2002). Faculty diversity: Too little for too long. *Harvard Magazine, 104*(4), 33–37. Retrieved from http://www.harvard-magazine.com/on-line/030218.html
Turner, C. S. V., & Myers, S. L., Jr. (2000). *Faculty of color in academe: Bittersweet success.* Needham Heights, MA: Allyn and Bacon.
Winborne, W. (2007, November). *Managing workforce diversity: A necessity in today's market.* Speech presented at The Human Rights Commission of Orange County, New Windsor, NY.

JERLANDO F. L. JACKSON *is the Vilas Distinguished Professor of higher education, and director and chief research scientist for Wisconsin's Equity and Inclusion Laboratory (Wei LAB) at the University of Wisconsin-Madison.*

ELIZABETH M. O'CALLAGHAN *is a lecturer in the Department of Educational Leadership and Policy Analysis at the University of Wisconsin-Madison.*

RAUL A. LEON *is an assistant professor of higher education at Eastern Michigan University.*

NEW DIRECTIONS FOR INSTITUTIONAL RESEARCH • DOI: 10.1002/ir

1

This chapter examines glass ceiling effects through the metric of salary equity.

Using Salary as a Measure of Glass Ceiling Effects: Lessons for Institutional Researchers

Vicki J. Rosser, Ketevan Mamiseishvili

Glass ceiling effects have been at the center of controversy within academia for years. No topic is more sensitive or anxiety-inducing than salary-equity issues, namely how salaries are fairly calculated according to faculty members' comparative worth for their work and productivity experiences. Salaries are among the most manipulated and measured variables (Hearn, 1999), with little consistency within and among disciplines, institutional types, colleges, and departments. As such, Cotter, Hermsen, Ovadia, and Vanneman (2001, pp. 657–661) provide four equity glass ceiling criteria that warrant investigation. This chapter filters these criteria through the discourse of current issues in higher education as they relate to glass ceiling effects on salary levels. The four criteria concern: (a) differences not explained by other job-relevant characteristics of the employee (e.g., experience, performance, and productivity); (b) greater differences at higher levels of an outcome than at lower levels (e.g., academic rank and tenure status); (c) inequalities in the prospects for advancement into higher levels, not merely the proportions of each gender or race currently at those higher levels (e.g., promotion and salary increases); and (d) inequalities that increase over the course of a career (e.g., cumulative impact of entry salaries, position, and compression).

Given these four criteria, this chapter will first highlight methodological considerations, including data use and research techniques that best facilitate an understanding of faculty members' salaries. Second, it will provide key institutional decision makers with useful profile characteristics and guidelines to contextualize the need for and the proposed use of salary-equity policies.

New Directions for Institutional Research, no. 159 © 2014 Wiley Periodicals, Inc.
Published online in Wiley Online Library (wileyonlinelibrary.com) • DOI: 10.1002/ir.20050

13

Salary-Equity Studies: Methodological Considerations

In the past four decades, numerous studies have focused on examining and explaining salary differentials. Since the mid-1970s, with the increased availability of multi-institution and national salary data, researchers have begun to employ sophisticated methodological approaches to provide accurate estimates of salary gaps (Barbezat, 2002). Consequently, the use and application of advanced statistical procedures allowed researchers to ask more complicated questions regarding salary equity. Over the past four decades, institutional researchers have devoted considerable attention to three primary methodological issues when designing salary-equity studies: who to study, what variables to include in the model, and what data analysis techniques to use (Barbezat, 2002; Ferber & Loeb, 2002; Luna, 2006; Toutkoushian & Hoffman, 2002). The section that follows will address these three considerations and provide an overview of findings from relevant faculty salary-equity studies.

Sample Selection in Salary-Equity Studies. The first important factor that researchers have considered is who should be included in salary-equity studies. The most frequent disagreements on the subject often concern the inclusion of part-time, temporary, and/or non-tenure-track faculty in samples (Luna, 2006). Some researchers believe that these individuals should be included in analyses on the premise that women are disproportionately overrepresented in nontraditional faculty appointments. As such, they argue that it is just as important to estimate and correct pay disparities for part-time, temporary, and non-tenure-track faculty members as for traditional, tenure-track faculty (Hamermesh, 1996). On the other hand, others contend that these groups are distinctive, and the inclusion of part-time, temporary, and/or non-tenure-track faculty in the study will lead to biased results (Snyder, Hyer, & McLaughlin, 1994). Luna (2006) concludes that courts tend to agree with the latter argument, namely that those with nonregular appointments ought to be regarded as separate from full-time faculty.

Variable Selection in Salary-Equity Studies. In addition to the question of who should be included in the studies, researchers also disagree on what variables should be accounted for in their analyses. Variable selection is crucial in salary-equity studies. In order to correctly estimate how much of the unexplained pay disparity exists between groups of faculty, differences in background and qualifications need to be accounted for (Toutkoushian & Hoffman, 2002). Thus, determining whether and to what extent gender discrimination exists in salary depends on the predictors that are included in a given analysis (Becker & Toutkoushian, 2003; Boudreau et al., 1997; Luna, 2007). After reviewing 24 faculty salary-equity studies, Becker and Toutkoushian (2003) identified the following variables as commonly used predictors in salary models: seniority, years in current rank, education, research productivity, administrative experience, and field.

Ferber and Loeb (2002) discuss the challenges in identifying potential explanatory variables that should be included in institutional salary-equity studies, such as experience, training, discipline, merit, productivity, and rank. Using data from full-time faculty ranks of assistant to full professor at four-year institutions in the state of Illinois, they demonstrated how the omission or inclusion of key variables—productivity and academic rank in particular—could affect the selection of individuals for salary-equity review. Their investigations consequently suggest that the inclusion of rank and the omission of productivity might be appropriate for investigating unexplained pay differences for all faculty members at an institution. When identifying a particular subset of faculty for salary adjustment review though, information about both productivity and rank must be considered together.

The overview of salary-equity studies suggests that the inclusion of academic rank as a variable in such analyses has been the most contested issue in these debates. Some researchers have favored omitting the rank variable from analyses on two assumptions. The first considers that the process of awarding rank may be influenced by institutional biases, and the second proposes that the inclusion of this gender-correlated variable could diminish existing salary differences according to gender (Moore, 1993). Alternatively, some researchers support the inclusion of rank in salary gender-equity studies (Becker & Toutkoushian, 2003; Boudreau et al., 1997). For example, Boudreau and collegues (1997) present two illustrations to demonstrate that the omission of faculty rank as a predictor can lead to inaccurate conclusions. Becker and Toutkoushian's (2003) study also argues that exclusion of the rank variable results in biased gender coefficients because "the effects of the omitted rank variable are captured in the error term, which is then correlated with the included gender variable" (p. 6).

Yet another contested issue is the omission of market discipline—typical factors in faculty salary studies (Herzog, 2008; Luna, 2007). Salary studies (Bellas, 1997; Herzog, 2008; Luna, 2007; Umbach, 2007) have included various types of measures to capture market differences in faculty pay, such as categorical variables for disciplines, geographical location, and market ratio, which is defined as "the ratio of the discipline salary average to the aggregate salary average of all disciplines" (Luna, 2007, p. 2). Using data from 20 southeastern state system, four-year institutions, Luna's (2007) study concluded that the field in which faculty members are employed serves as a significant predictor of salary variability. Despite evidence suggesting that more females are choosing higher market disciplines than in the past, Luna (2007) reports that female faculty members are still disproportionately earning their degrees in disciplines with low market value, consequently earning lower salaries.

Another study, Umbach (2007), also explores to what extent labor market conditions of academic disciplines explain the gender-wage gap.

Based on the data from the 1999 National Study of Postsecondary Faculty (NSOPF:99) and the Survey of Earned Doctorates (SED), Umbach (2007) employed hierarchical linear modeling (HLM) to examine the effects of disciplinary and individual characteristics on academic salaries. The study found that, when controlling for human capital factors including experience, education, seniority, research productivity, and teaching, females earned about 8% less than males. When disciplinary labor market conditions and an individual discipline's structural characteristics were accounted for, however, the gap reduced to 6.8%, which equates to a $5,400 difference in annual salary. Additionally, faculty in female-dominated disciplines earned less than their counterparts in male-dominated disciplines.

Issues associated with variable omission and selection biases, especially with regard to career progression measures, present challenges to institutional research analysts in salary compensation studies as well. Specifically, these issues make it difficult for analysts to identify faculty who are genuinely underpaid. As a result, Herzog (2008) proposed a comprehensive four-step process to identify and control for some of these biases, for the sake of arriving at a more parsimonious salary adjustment model. Herzog's (2008) proposed faculty compensation model consists of the following four steps: (a) canonical correlation to detect biases related to personal attributes, such as gender, race/ethnicity, age, marital status, etc.; (b) binary logistic regression to detect biases in tenure award processes; (c) multinomial logistic regression to discover biases in rank promotion; and (d) multiple linear regression to identify inequities in faculty salary (p. 52). According to Herzog (2008), the first three steps are necessary to determine what personal and professional faculty characteristics are related to pay inequities. After identifying what variables should be included or excluded from the analysis, researchers can proceed with the final step in the compensation model to determine cases of salary adjustment as well as the amount of said adjustment (Herzog, 2008).

Choice of Data Analysis Techniques in Salary-Equity Studies. The third and final methodological issue to consider in salary-equity studies is the choice of an appropriate data analysis technique. Earlier studies have tended to examine mean differences in male and female faculty salaries, mostly within a single discipline or rank, failing to take into account other factors that might have affected faculty salaries. But Loeb's (2003) review of salary-equity methodological approaches indicates that the studies range from simple estimations of salary means to complex statistical analyses.

One concern that Loeb (2003) raises in regard to using Ordinary Least Squares (OLS) in salary-equity studies, however, is that it treats all observations as independent from each other, ignoring the data's nested nature. Typically, faculty members in salary studies do not act independently of one another, but are clustered within their departments, disciplines, or institutions. If this clustering of observations is ignored, it might lead to inaccurate estimates (Loeb, 2003; Perna, 2003; Umbach, 2007). In turn, Loeb recommends the use of HLM to compensate for this shortcoming, and, up until now, few studies have applied the technique to salary data. Umbach's (2007) study, as previously mentioned, is in fact one of the first studies to employ HLM to examine the effects of a broad range of individual and disciplinary characteristics on faculty salary. Additionally, Loeb argues that HLM presents clear advantages, the most obvious of which is that it accounts for the clustering of observations within disciplines or institutions, providing unbiased significance tests (Loeb, 2003; Umbach, 2007). In addition, HLM accurately determines what disciplinary or institutional characteristics are responsible for gender-based earning inequalities (Haberfeld, Semyonov, & Addi, 1998).

While no salary-equity studies method can be labeled as indisputably superior, researchers have proposed a range of alternatives for analyzing these data (Bereman & Scott, 1991; Hagedorn, 1996; Herzog, 2008; Loeb, 2003; Toutkoushian & Hoffman, 2002). For example, Bereman and Scott suggest using the compa-ratio, a technique widely used in the corporate sector to detect gender biases in faculty salaries. Calculated by dividing the actual faculty pay by the midpoint salary, or the average salary by rank and discipline for a specific faculty group (Bereman & Scott, 1991), the compa-ratio is an efficient way to determine whether an individual is paid above or below the midpoint. By analyzing salary data from a Midwestern university using both OLS and compa-ratio techniques, Bereman and Scott illustrated that the compa-ratio could effectively identify individual cases for salary review and adjustment. They concluded that, because of its simplicity and ease of utility, compa-ratio can provide useful information about institutions' salary level in relation to national or regional academic labor markets.

Individual growth modeling (IGM) is another effective technique that can be applied to studying changes in faculty salary over time. Bellas, Ritchey, and Parmer (2001) used this method to observe gender differences in salary and salary growth rates between 1985 and 1995 using a sample of 306 faculty members at a large public research university. Three important findings emerged from their study that could inform policy discussions on salary equity. First, after controlling for a range of factors, the study found a gap of about $2,000 between female and male faculty members in the base year of 1985. Second, the results suggested that, over the ten-year period, women showed higher rates of salary increases than men. Finally, the study indicated that faculty members with higher salary growth were more likely to leave their institutions. Equally as important, the study demonstrated that IGM could be used effectively in conjunction with longitudinal data to capture "the dynamic nature of gender differences in faculty salaries and the mechanisms that contribute to these differences" (Bellas et al., 2001, p. 179).

A number of factors affect the choice of methodology for salary data analysis, including how a given institution discriminates. Toutkoushian and Hoffman (2002) provide three different scenarios of salary discrimination, each of which requires the use of a different technique—that is, single-, two-, or three-equation methods. The single-equation method, the most commonly used in institutional salary-equity studies, assumes that an institution discriminates by overpaying all members of a specific employee group, for example, all male faculty members. Toutkoushian and Hoffman (2002) criticize this method as limiting because "it restricts each of the independent variables to having the same impact on salary for workers in either group" (p. 74). In contrast, a two-equation model allows the independent variable to have differential impacts on salaries of employees in two different groups. Alternatively, when an institution discriminates by simultaneously overpaying its employees in one group and underpaying individuals in another group, Toutkoushian and Hoffman (2002) suggest using a three-equation method to measure the unexplained wage differentials. Despite the complexities associated with computing multiple-equation models and assumptions pertaining to certain institutional practices of discrimination, the authors recommend these models as best practices for measuring unexplained wage gaps in institutional salary-equity studies.

Review of Relevant Research Findings

So far, this chapter has identified several methodological issues researchers encounter when designing salary-equity studies. This review demonstrates that, over the past four decades, progress has been made in advancing methodological approaches to more accurately estimate existing wage gaps. A larger question remains, however. How much progress has been made in actually reducing wage gaps and eliminating salary discrimination in higher education institutions? Using data from NSOPF:99, Toutkoushian and Conley (2005) provide empirical support for the contention that progress has been made, concluding that there has been a decrease in pay disparities between male and female faculty members, especially at doctoral-level and liberal arts institutions. But the study also reveals that, on average, even after accounting for a broad range of human capital and structural characteristics, such as experience, education, field, rank, and institutional type, a 4%–6% gender gap in faculty salaries persists.

The fact that the wage gap is smaller among younger cohorts of female and male faculty can also be interpreted as a sign of progress. Using the data from two NSOPF surveys, 1988 and 1993, Toutkoushian (1998) found that the unexplained wage gap among faculty of younger age groups in 1992 was smaller than that of the older faculty age groups. Similar conclusions can be drawn from Perna's (2001a) study that examined sex differences in salary among six cohorts of faculty using the data from NSOPF:93. The study found that, after controlling for human capital investment, productivity, and structural characteristics, there were no differences in male–female faculty salaries for new assistant professors, associate professors with 7–12 years of experience, and full professors with 13–24 years of experience. On the other hand, women faculty earned 8% less at the rank of assistant professor with 3–6 years of experience, 9% less at the associate professor rank with 13–24 years of experience, and 6% less as full professors with more than 20 years of experience in comparison to their male counterparts in the same cohorts. According to Perna (2001a) then, "the absence of unexplained sex differences in salaries among the 'younger' faculty at each academic rank is a sign of progress" (p. 301).

These studies should be read as definite signs of progress, but much work remains to eliminate pay disparities. Gaps persist not only in base salaries but also in supplemental incomes, which further disproportionately benefit male faculty who show bigger gains in overall earnings (Perna, 2002). Furthermore, even when no evidence exists of inequitable treatment at the time of hire, significant gender-based pay disparities emerge over time (Porter, Toutkoushian, & Moore, 2008). Moreover, Toutkoushian and Conley (2005) argue that salary studies using national data only explain half of salary variation, even after controlling for a wide range of personal, disciplinary, and institutional characteristics.

Salary-Equity Policies: Profiles and Guidelines

Tensions relating to salary often play out in three general ways: parity, equity, and longevity (Rosser, 2009). Parity involves salary equivalences across groups, while equity refers to principles of fairness and justice in the context of correcting or supplementing disparities. Longevity, on the other hand, encompasses the cumulative impact of individuals' time and experience within an organization or throughout their career. Studies focused on longevity examine those areas that create the most tension regarding salary equity. The individual profile characteristics, more commonly referred to as demographic variables, that most often affect salary equity include: sex, age, disability, race, religion, national origin, marital status, and sexual orientation.

While common sense dictates that full professors should be paid more than associates and associates more than assistants, intrarank salary variation is another matter. There is considerable debate whenever rank is used as a control variable because women and ethnic minorities tend to be overrepresented in junior positions. As such, the policy issues and institutional concerns that comprise the relationship between women and lower salary levels warrant greater empirical understanding. The gender salary gap may be reduced in some cases over time when women attain full professor status (Toutkoushian & Conley, 2005), although women tend to be more represented at junior ranks, so their numbers are sparse at the higher level (Perna, 2001a, 2001b).

Another area of concern is the interplay between individuals' work status, whether part-time or full-time, and their tenure status, namely tenure-track, non-tenure-track, tenured, or untenured. Research continues to show that the majority of women and ethnic minority faculty members are overrepresented in early-career ranks and are nontenured. Similarly, type of institution—for example, research university, liberal arts college, or community college—might also produce a direct or indirect impact on salary levels (American Association of University Professors, 2008; Fairweather, 1993; Perna, 2003). In terms of direct impact, pay levels are clearly different among institutional types, but indirect glass ceiling disparities often occur with respect to gender in the same institutional type.

Numerous scholars have identified a wide range of issues requiring further empirical work, specifically around the career prospects for ethnic minority women (Ards, Brintnall, & Woodard, 1997; Johnsrud & Sadao, 1998; Lee, 2002; Perna, 2001b, 2003; Porter et al., 2008), as well as pipeline problems, market forces, and chilly climates (Turner, Myers, & Creswell, 1999). While some studies find little connection or effect between Caucasian and ethnic minority women (Cotter et al., 2001), previous empirical work has shown that women and ethnic minorities have been, and continue to be, underpaid over time, particularly among individuals securing their first academic position (Clery & Christopher, 2008). The impact of lower-than-average entry-level salaries may be extremely detrimental to women and ethnic minorities over the course of their careers.

Just as parity and equity are important to the quality of faculty work life, issues surrounding institutional longevity are critical as well. Longevity, rarely discussed within salary-equity policies, encompasses salary compression issues for those senior faculty members who have chosen to stay at one institution. Colleagues often refer to this commitment as a "loyalty tax" in which faculty members are penalized for their loyalty to stay at their current institutions rather than securing base salary increases elsewhere.

As noted throughout the relevant empirical literature, there remains a need for clear and consistent salary-equity policies. While numerous tensions continue to exist throughout academia regarding the fair and equitable nature of these policies, discussions must continue to progress for the sake of enhancing faculty members' professional and institutional work lives. To guide these policy discussions, Hearn (1999) provides nine broad criteria upon which salary systems can be judged: (a) deemphasizing the external marketplace, (b) adopting the core-salary approach, (c) tying annual salary changes more directly to annual performance, (d) standardizing salaries in association with career ladders, (e) decoupling merit evaluation for salary increases and faculty development efforts, (f) pursuing internal consistency in the determination of salaries, (g) welcoming faculty participation in determination of merit-based increases, (h) facilitating public scrutiny of salaries, and (i) evaluating teaching and public service as criteria for salary adjustment. These criteria provide a minimum overview of primary parameters for institutional researchers to examine, encompassing the full range of faculty members' profile and demographic characteristics used in equity analyses.

Faculty salaries, and, more specifically, equitable salary compensation, remain an important aspect of academia and the professional work life. Accordingly, the annual salaries for all faculty members should be consistently monitored, assessed, and evaluated within an established time frame mutually agreed upon by faculty and administration. While the advancement of methodological procedures is beginning to catch up with questions regarding salary and equity issues, future research is required to uncover what remains unknown about salary inequities in higher education in order to improve practices and policies involving salary-equity issues.

References

American Association of University Professors. (2008). *Where are the priorities? The annual report on the economic status of the profession, 2007–2008.* Washington, DC: Author.

Ards, S., Brintnall, M., & Woodard, M. (1997). The road to tenure and beyond for African American political scientists. *The Journal of Negro Education, 66*(2), 159–171.

Barbezat, D. A. (2002). History of pay equity studies. In R. K. Toutkoushian (Ed.), *New Directions for Institutional Research: No. 115. Conducting salary-equity studies: Alternative approaches to research* (pp. 9–40). San Francisco, CA: Jossey-Bass.

Becker, W. E., & Toutkoushian, R. K. (2003). Measuring gender bias in the salaries of tenured faculty members. In R. K. Toutkoushian (Ed.), *New Directions for Institutional Research: No. 117. Unresolved issues in salary-equity studies* (pp. 5–20). San Francisco, CA: Jossey-Bass.

Bellas, M. L. (1997). Disciplinary differences in faculty salaries: Does gender bias play a role? *The Journal of Higher Education, 68*(3), 299–321.

Bellas, M. L., Ritchey, P. N., & Parmer, P. (2001). Gender differences in the salaries and salary growth rates of university faculty: An exploratory study. *Sociological Perspectives, 44*(2), 163–187.

Bereman, N. A., & Scott, J. A. (1991). Using the compa-ratio to detect gender bias in faculty studies. *The Journal of Higher Education, 62*(5), 556–569.

Boudreau, N., Sullivan, J., Balzer, W., Ryan, A. M., Yonker, R., Thorsteinson, T., & Hutchinson, P. (1997). Should faculty rank be included as a predictor variable in studies of gender equity university faculty salaries? *Research in Higher Education, 38*(3), 297–312.

Clery, S. B., & Christopher, B. L. (2008). Faculty salaries: 2006–2007. In *The 2008 NEA almanac of higher education* (pp. 7–28). Washington, DC: The National Education Association.

Cotter, D. A., Hermsen, J. M., Ovadia, S., & Vanneman, R. (2001). The glass ceiling effect. *Social Forces, 80*(2), 655–681.

Fairweather, J. S. (1993). Faculty reward structures: Toward institutional and professional homogenization. *Research in Higher Education, 34*(5), 603–623.

Ferber, M. A., & Loeb, J. W. (2002). Issues in conducting an institutional salary-equity study. In R. K. Toutkoushian (Ed.), *New Directions for Institutional Research: No. 115. Conducting salary-equity studies: Alternative approaches to research* (pp. 41–70). San Francisco, CA: Jossey-Bass.

Haberfeld, Y., Semyonov, M., & Addi, A. (1998). A hierarchical linear model for estimating gender-based earnings differentials. *Work and Occupations*, 25(1), 97–112.

Hagedorn, L. S. (1996). Wage equity and female faculty satisfaction: The role of wage differentials in a job satisfaction casual model. *Research in Higher Education*, 37(5), 569–598.

Hamermesh, D. (1996). Not so bad: The annual report on the economic status of the profession. *Academe*, 82, 104–108.

Hearn, J. C. (1999). Pay and performance in the university: An examination of faculty salaries. *The Review of Higher Education*, 22(4), 391–410.

Herzog, S. (2008). A four-step faculty compensation model: From equity analysis to adjustment. In N. A. Valcik (Ed.), *New Directions for Institutional Research: No. 140. Using financial and personnel data in a changing world for institutional research* (pp. 49–64). San Francisco, CA: Jossey-Bass.

Johnsrud, L. K., & Sadao, K. C. (1998). The common experience of 'Otherness': Ethnic and racial minority faculty. *The Review of Higher Education*, 21(4), 315–342.

Lee, S. M. (2002). Do Asian American faculty face a glass ceiling in higher education? *American Educational Research Journal*, 39(3), 695–724.

Loeb, J. W. (2003). Hierarchical linear modeling in salary-equity studies. In R. K. Toutkoushian (Ed.), *New Directions for Institutional Research: No. 117. Unresolved issues in salary-equity studies* (pp. 69–96). San Francisco, CA: Jossey-Bass.

Luna, A. L. (2006). Faculty salary equity cases: Combining statistics with the law. *The Journal of Higher Education*, 77(2), 193–224.

Luna, A. L. (2007). Using a market ratio factor in faculty salary equity studies. *Association for Institutional Research (AIR) Professional File*, 103, 1–16.

Moore, N. (1993). Faculty salary equity: Issues in regression model selection. *Research in Higher Education*, 34(1), 107–126.

Perna, L. W. (2001a). Sex differences in faculty salaries: A cohort analysis. *The Review of Higher Education*, 24(3), 283–307.

Perna, L. W. (2001b). Sex and race differences in faculty tenure and promotion. *Research in Higher Education*, 42(5), 541–567.

Perna, L. W. (2002). Sex differences in the supplemental earnings of college and university faculty. *Research in Higher Education*, 43(1), 31–58.

Perna, L. W. (2003). The status of women and minorities among community college faculty. *Research in Higher Education*, 44(2), 205–240.

Porter, S. R., Toutkoushian, R. K., & Moore, J. V., III. (2008). Pay inequities for recently hired faculty, 1988–2004. *The Review of Higher Education*, 31(4), 465–487.

Rosser, V. J. (2009). Important issues facing support professionals in higher education: The key issues survey. In *The 2009 NEA almanac of higher education* (pp. 93–97). Washington, DC: The National Education Association.

Snyder, J. K., Hyer, P. B., & McLaughlin, G. W. (1994). Faculty salary equity: Issues and options. *Research in Higher Education*, 35(1), 1–19.

Toutkoushian, R. K. (1998). Sex matters less for younger faculty: Evidence of disaggregate pay disparities from the 1988 and 1993 NCES surveys. *Economics of Education Review*, 17(1), 55–71.

Toutkoushian, R. K., & Conley, V. M. (2005). Progress for women in academe, yet inequities persist: Evidence from NSOPF:99. *Research in Higher Education*, 46(1), 1–28.

Toutkoushian, R. K., & Hoffman, E. P. (2002). Alternatives for measuring the unexplained wage gap. In R. K. Toutkoushian (Ed.), *New Directions for Institutional Research: No. 115. Conducting salary-equity studies: Alternative approaches to research* (pp. 71–90). San Francisco, CA: Jossey-Bass.

Turner, C. S. V., Myers, S. L., Jr., & Creswell, J. W. (1999). Exploring underrepresentation: The case of faculty of color in the Midwest. *The Journal of Higher Education, 70*(1), 27–59.

Umbach, P. D. (2007). Gender equity in the academic labor market: An analysis of academic disciplines. *Research in Higher Education, 48*(2), 169–192.

VICKI J. ROSSER is a professor of higher education at the University of Nevada–Las Vegas.

KETEVAN MAMISEISHVILI is an associate professor of higher education leadership at the University of Arkansas.

2

This chapter highlights the importance of qualitative approaches to studying the glass ceiling in contrast to exclusively quantitative measures.

Using Critical Interpretive Lenses to Examine Glass Ceiling Effects Through Qualitative Research

Lori D. Patton, Chayla M. Haynes

In this chapter, we not only engage the difficulties associated with defining the glass ceiling but also endeavor toward two goals. First, we review general literature that has examined the glass ceiling. Then we discuss the importance of qualitative research in advancing knowledge about the glass ceiling. In order to add greater dimensionality to existing studies of the glass ceiling, we explore two critical interpretive lenses employed in this research. Finally, considerations are offered for future study, specifically how qualitative research framed through these lenses can be employed to examine important issues associated with the glass ceiling.

Glass Ceiling Background and Literature Review

Discourse surrounding the glass ceiling has been present in both academic and nonacademic arenas since 1978, coinciding with a speech to the Women's Action Alliance that made reference to those "invisible barriers to women's career advancement" (Carnes, Morrissey, & Geller, 2008, p. 1453). Unfair hiring practices in the corporate sector drew attention throughout the late 1970s, and the glass ceiling metaphor was used to communicate the grim reality that "despite the entry of women into nearly all fields traditionally occupied by men, women remain virtually nonexistent or present in token numbers in elite leadership positions" (Carnes et al., 2008, p. 1453). Today, women continue to be underrepresented in corporate leadership roles.

Eventually, the glass ceiling garnered the attention of the U.S. government, and as a result, the Federal Glass Ceiling Commission was established. It quickly acknowledged the existence of the glass ceiling, a barrier that "prohibited the advancement of women and people of color in

New Directions for Institutional Research, no. 159 © 2014 Wiley Periodicals, Inc.
Published online in Wiley Online Library (wileyonlinelibrary.com) • DOI: 10.1002/ir.20051

25

the workplace" (Jackson & O'Callaghan, 2009, p. 462). Among the Commission's initial goals was to study those artificial advancement barriers that prevent minority groups' ascent into management and upper-level positions in corporate America. As a result of their investigation into this phenomenon, the Commission prepared and published four major reports, each citing and documenting the existence of glass ceilings for women and racial/ethnic minorities in the U.S. labor force.

The breadth of their reports characterized the glass ceiling as an "unseen, yet unbreachable barrier that keeps minorities and women from rising to the upper rungs of the corporate ladder, regardless of their qualifications or achievements" (Cotter, Hermsen, Ovadia, & Vanneman, 2001, p. 656). In an effort to address those who were skeptical of the existence of the glass ceiling and its effects, Elacqua, Beehr, Hansen, & Webster (2009) conducted a study that examined female managers' perceptions of workplace advancement barriers. They concluded that interpersonal and situational factors—namely, the extent to which managers serve as mentors, the prominence of an "old boys' network," and potential connections with organizational decision makers—not only contributed to employees' views about the persistence of the glass ceiling but also affected whether or not individuals were promoted in the organization.

Moreover, Elacqua and others (2009) argued that mentorship—or the lack thereof—played a sizeable role in employees' perceptions of differential treatment. According to their findings, women are less likely to excel in their careers because they have fewer "mentors, informal networks, influential colleagues, role models, and stretch assignments" (p. 286). The relative lack of valuable mentoring relationships among women employees is exacerbated by the tendency for people to prefer mentoring relationships with others of the same gender. Additionally, the existence of an "old boys' network" and the associated preferential treatment that often arises from relationships with powerful decision makers presents another significant obstacle for women, who are less likely to establish these important links to their more visible male counterparts (Elacqua et al., 2009).

The Elacqua study, however, emphasizes important situational factors of a different nature: objective hiring standards and perceptions of women managers who have held their positions long enough to be considered serious candidates for promotion. The findings suggest that female employees associate the glass ceiling with an observed pattern of promotions seemingly unrelated to objective hiring standards. This differential treatment leads many to demand objective performance-related criteria. With few women in the "promotion pipeline," this problem is compounded. Study findings indicate that women believe their female counterparts to be next in line for high-level management positions if they are already in management positions or receiving developmental assistance (Elacqua et al., 2009).

The glass ceiling metaphor does not fully capture the extent to which discriminatory practices impede the advancement of women and people

NEW DIRECTIONS FOR INSTITUTIONAL RESEARCH • DOI: 10.1002/ir

of color in the workplace. Taking note of the organizational changes in social, demographic, legal, and economic contexts since the 1980s, Bendl and Schmidt (2010) contend that the glass ceiling metaphor is no longer sufficient for describing those institutional inequalities that women and minorities face. Instead, they propose a new metaphor, the "firewall," to describe these barriers. Bendl and Schmidt (2010) argue, "It's the whole structure of the organizations in which we work; the foundation, the beams, the walls, and the very air that act as impediments. Barriers to advancement are not just above, they are all around" (p. 613). Although the authors do not suggest discarding the glass ceiling metaphor altogether, they contend that a firewall better captures the subtleties and hidden forces of workplace discrimination.

While both metaphors illuminate discriminatory behaviors, each conveys different meanings. The glass ceiling may offer a structural view of the institutional status quo of discrimination, or "having discrimination," but the firewall offers a more process-oriented view of discrimination, or "doing discrimination" (Bendl & Schmidt, 2010, p. 629). This latter metaphor better communicates how discrimination is performed and reproduced in today's organizations.

The glass ceiling terminology has evolved over the years to reflect differences in how effects have manifested in relation to impact, population, and scarcity of resources while still maintaining the metaphor's core aspects. Elacqua and others (2009) use the term "glass cliff," for example, to describe the promotion of women into upper-level positions in which workplace instability, failure, and job loss remain all-too-common outcomes. Moreover, the metaphor implies that women are required to endure greater risk than their male counterparts, for they are often forced to accept unwanted positions if they have aspirations of advancing up the corporate ladder. Livers and Lewis (2009), alternatively, introduce the term "concrete ceiling" to identify the impenetrability of those barriers that prevent black women from rising to the upper echelons of corporate America, while Jackson and O'Callaghan (2009) use the idea of the "double whammy" to convey the experiences of black women who occupy two minority identities. Additionally, Carnes et al. (2008) apply the term "sticky floor" to describe the employment conditions of female physicians who receive fewer resources and promotions than male physicians at the start of their careers.

Whether conceptualized as a glass ceiling, firewall, glass cliff, concrete ceiling, double whammy, or sticky floor, the effects of workplace discrimination on women and people of color are long-standing and far-reaching (Cotter et al., 2001; Elacqua et al., 2009; Jackson & O'Callaghan, 2009). The Elacqua study further indicated that workplace discrimination often leaves women and minorities with little recourse, diminishing ambitions or causing outright departures from organizations. In order to prevent these outcomes, additional research must examine the glass ceiling's differential effects.

Preoccupations With the Glass Ceiling

The literature reviewed above prompts a discussion about some of the common preoccupations in glass ceiling research. One preoccupation concerns metaphors, which may well be central to language and understanding but are often overused or inappropriately used in relation to the glass ceiling. The use of the metaphor can be especially problematic when it is employed to describe phenomena that are not necessarily reflective of personal experiences; there is a difference between applying metaphor to unearth realities about the lives of individuals and using it for the sake of euphemism. Cotter and others (2001) explain:

> If the 'glass ceiling' is intended merely as a more colorful phrase to describe what we already mean by gender or racial inequality, then we are proliferating concepts that may ease our communication with the public, but do little to advance our work as analysts of the causes of inequality. (p. 656)

Some metaphors may tickle the imagination but contribute very little in terms of prompting substantive or transformative changes in oppressive organizational systems.

The second preoccupation involves a tendency to define the glass ceiling in a finite manner as opposed to capturing the term's breadth through a multiplicity of definitions. While a host of definitions have been leveraged to describe the glass ceiling and its effects, defining it remains futile because the phenomenon is continually reshaping itself from context to context. Moreover, operationalization has tended to defer to existing definitions that others have already used. Alternatively, the term is applied without any context (Jackson & O'Callaghan, 2009).

Finally, many often mistakenly assume the glass ceiling to be synonymous with gender. This linkage is problematic for two reasons. Although gender clearly remains an important example of the glass ceiling, this association prompts researchers to focus overwhelmingly on the experiences of women—to the exclusion of other cases. Little is known about how and to what extent the glass ceiling affects men or transgendered individuals. Such an exclusive focus on gendered identities ignores other salient identities and systems of oppression rooted in racism, heterosexism, and classism. Notably, there is a substantial lack of research that attempts to parse the intersections between race/ethnicity and gender with regard to glass ceiling effects (Jackson & O'Callaghan, 2009).

How Can Qualitative Research Be Useful?

Few articles in the canon of glass ceiling literature employ qualitative research methods. Jackson and O'Callaghan's (2009) taxonomy of this literature uncovered that of 66 publications concerning glass ceiling effects,

NEW DIRECTIONS FOR INSTITUTIONAL RESEARCH • DOI: 10.1002/ir

only 9.1% were grounded in qualitative methods. Yet these qualitative perspectives on glass ceiling effects remain central to providing a more nuanced understanding of how these phenomena affect various populations.

A number of scholars have expressed support for the use of qualitative research. Referencing qualitative research as a tool for uncovering nuanced experiences, Merriam (2002) explains that several themes become prevalent through the use of such methods, among them a focus on how individuals construct meaning. Additionally, qualitative research is concerned with naturalistic, context-specific inquiry, requiring interpretations and meaning to emerge from the field as opposed to scholars' own prior understandings (Bogdan & Biklen, 2006; Merriam, 2002). Qualitative research compels researchers to assess phenomena from the perspective of those who experience it.

Given that qualitative approaches remain a rarity in research examining glass ceiling effects, it is important to note how it can specifically contribute to future research in this area. While quantitative research provides useful tools for analyzing many research questions, the heavy emphasis on systematizing observations and generalizability may sometimes simplify, ignore, or subvert the particular contours of individual experiences.

Researchers have a wide array of qualitative approaches at their disposal that can be used to critique, examine, disrupt, and reveal glass ceiling effects, most relevant of which include narrative studies, case studies, and ethnographic studies. According to Merriam (2002), narrative studies are integral because their data entail first-person accounts of individual experience, retold in story form. For example, a researcher might seek to identify how women faculty at three separate institutions, all of whom have retired at the associate professor level, have experienced the glass ceiling throughout their careers. Specifically, a narrative approach could be applied by conducting a life history or biography to capture the personal voices of these women with the goal of revealing how they came to understand the barriers that prevented them from achieving full professor status. Conversely, a different narrative study could illuminate the stories of women faculty who have earned full professor status, allowing them to articulate the strategies and experiences facilitating their promotion.

Case studies can also be instrumental in studying glass ceiling effects through attention to specific settings or contexts (Creswell, 2007). The inherent flexibility of this methodology allows for the use of multiple data sources, such as interviews, documents, and observations, to respond to research questions. A researcher, for instance, could uncover extremely valuable findings from a study that analyzes the experiences of women faculty from a single institution who retired at the associate professor level. These women could conceivably represent a range of departments and disciplines, offering rich perspectives about their career trajectories. Their shared letters and other correspondence might be used in a comprehensive document analysis. Instances of institutional discrimination, workplace culture, and the nature of impenetrable advancement networks could all surface in a case study approach, helping to clarify possible avenues for rectifying glass ceiling effects or, alternatively, illuminating strategies to help employees maneuver around institutional barriers.

Another tradition of qualitative research, ethnography, focuses on the interactions over time of multiple people in a group setting and a larger cultural context (Creswell, 2007). Ethnographers engage in extensive observations and interviews to "study the meaning of the behavior, the language, and the interaction among members of the culture-sharing group" (Creswell, 2007, p. 69). Researchers who engage in ethnography, subsequently, might wish to study how full professors—often White men—make decisions regarding who else has the qualifications and is deserving of this status. Findings from these data could reveal hegemonic practices and ideologies responsible for the existence of glass ceiling effects, furthering our understanding of how the glass ceiling is perpetuated and reproduced.

What is offered here is a snapshot of qualitative approaches that can be used to guide glass ceiling effects research. Of course, a host of other methodologies can enhance this line of research. While qualitative efforts are sorely needed to unearth the causal mechanisms and the nuances of glass ceiling effects, equally important is how qualitative researchers approach such problems. They must be conscious as to how such research is framed and how these decisions influence the types of questions asked and the glass ceiling issues investigated.

Using Interpretive Frameworks to Examine Glass Ceiling Effects

This section describes two interpretive frameworks that have the capacity to shape and advance knowledge regarding glass ceiling effects. These frameworks are critical because they determine what research questions are asked, what types of data are collected and from what sources, how data are analyzed, and ultimately how data are interpreted and reported. Additionally, these interpretive lenses are integral to examining social, cultural, educational, and political issues that disproportionately affect the lives and experiences of "minoritized" populations. In contrast to the term "minority," the word "minoritized" draws attention to the "relative prestige of languages and cultures" as well as the conditions of social interactions at both national and international levels (Mukherjee, Mukherjee, & Godard, 2006, p. 1). The term captures the historical legacy and present status of oppression, exclusion, and discrimination directed toward populations who experience racism, sexism, heterosexism, and/or classism.

The interpretive frameworks highlighted next are aimed at investigating issues and conditions that reproduce systems of dominance and oppression, ensure the inequitable distribution of resources and power, and silence the voices of the marginalized. Moreover, these frameworks are grounded in a social justice agenda that not only reveals salient issues but also calls for praxis.

NEW DIRECTIONS FOR INSTITUTIONAL RESEARCH • DOI: 10.1002/ir

Critical Race Theory. Critical Race Theory (CRT) offers a useful framework for examining glass ceiling effects, challenging and critiquing the manner in which race and racism operate (Bell, 1992; Delgado & Stefancic, 2001). Central to CRT is the premise that racism is embedded in social, political, and legal systems and institutions around which peoples' lives are shaped. Racism is wholly entrenched in society, and particularly in education, to the extent that it can be barely recognizable, making it extremely difficult to address (Delgado & Stefancic, 2001; Ladson-Billings & Tate, 1995).

Another central tenet of CRT is its continuous critique and deconstruction of "colorblind" ideologies. Valdes, Culp, and Harris (2002) explain that notions of colorblindness exist through the following beliefs: ignoring race will end racism, racism is individual in nature rather than systemic, and racism can be addressed without considering other types of oppression. Understanding colorblindness, then, is key to any discourse on glass ceiling effects because efforts to explain away inequities tend to perpetuate an unconscious disregard for the experiences of people of color, limiting accountability for systemic injustices, and blaming outcomes of racism on individuals or groups of color. In effect, such notions promote apathetic, subtle, and covert forms of racism (Forman, 2004).

Also important to CRT is its emphasis on White privilege, challenging the racially hegemonic status quo that standardizes White experience. This privilege undergirds the enactment of the glass ceiling. CRT also overlaps with the concept of interest convergence, best described by critical race theorists as incidents in which Black interests—as well as those of other racialized communities—converge with those of Whites. These advances are only tolerated, however, so long as they do not pose any threat to White privilege (Bell, 2000; Delgado, 1995). Such acts of interest convergence, which serve as temporary alliances rather than long-term, equitable solutions, pervade the policies and practices of higher education (Harper, Patton, & Wooden, 2009).

Lastly, CRT is articulated through the experiential knowledge of communities of color, often expressed through counterstories. Useful for their ability to connect critical consciousness and social relations, counterstories are considered by critical race theorists to be factual, valid, and empirically sound forms of evidence. Stock stories, for example, often privileged as objective truth, might suggest that the glass ceiling persists because women of color lack adequate preparation and qualifications to be senior leaders. Counterstories, on the other hand, might reveal that decision makers shift rules, requirements, and/or criteria for advancement in promotion situations. Solórzano and Yosso (2002) contend that the use of a CRT framework—and by extension, counterstories—in educational contexts is necessary because it "focuses on the experiences of students and communities of color to learn from their racialized experiences with oppression" (p. 156). Through the use of CRT and counterstorytelling, scholars recognize that appreciating the circumstances of underrepresented populations is best accomplished through listening to the experiences of people of color and bringing their stories to the foreground.

Intersectionality and Intersectional Frameworks. In discussing intersectionality, Hulko (2009) offers the following:

> Researching and writing about intersectionality and interlocking oppressions often require a blurring of any remaining lines of distinction between the personal and the professional because identity, oppression, and privilege are not sole abstract concepts; they have real, complex, and often-disputed meanings in our daily lives. (p. 44)

Hulko goes on to advocate for an intersectional perspective in examining diverse social identities. Other scholars have also recently offered perspectives on intersectionality in an attempt to capture the complexity of identity, with Few (2007) describing an "intersectionality matrix" as "a specific location where multiple systems of oppressions... conceal deliberate, marginalizing ideological maneuvers that define 'Otherness'" (p. 454).

Two critical concepts are important for understanding intersectionality as an interpretive framework: antiessentialism and standpoint. Antiessentialism might best be understood through Critical Race Feminism (CRF), another perspective within the larger framework of intersectionality. CRF encourages researchers to examine a variety of social institutions to explore the interactions of racially minoritized women within these contexts and to investigate the manner in which related inequities are reinforced and reproduced. Additionally, CRF challenges gendered and sexist systems that produce such inequities for women of color. CRF emerged from the exclusion that racially and ethnically minoritized women experienced at the hands of White women and racial/ethnic minoritized men in the legal profession.

In any case, scholars who incorporate an intersectional lens into qualitative research should challenge essentialism or the failure to acknowledge intragroup differences. Crenshaw (1991), a noted critical race feminist, touches upon the necessity of this commitment when she states that intersectional frameworks attempt to disrupt the general failure to acknowledge intersectional identities within feminist and antiracist discourses, resulting in the silencing of women of color. Crenshaw explains:

> Feminist efforts to politicize experiences of women and antiracist efforts to politicize experiences of people of color have frequently proceeded as though the issues and experiences they each detail occur on mutually exclusive terrains. Although racism and sexism readily intersect in the lives of real people, they seldom do in feminist and antiracist practices.... When the practices expound identity as woman or person of color as an either/or proposition, they relegate the identity of women of color to a location that resists telling. (p. 1242)

NEW DIRECTIONS FOR INSTITUTIONAL RESEARCH • DOI: 10.1002/ir

The tendency, then, to rely on essentialism is problematic for several reasons. Efforts toward group unification inevitably benefit only select members of the group. Similarly, these endeavors fail to reflect unique and individual perspectives within the group, and although claims of consensus purport to speak for everyone, in fact they represent the conscious efforts of one group to situate itself as a collective of several diverse perspectives (Harris, 1990). Finally, these dynamics are often initiated and directed by individuals who believe they wield the most power, and as a result dominate the discussion.

The second concept necessary for understanding intersectionality is standpoint, which refers to whether individuals are situated at the center or the margins of social groups depending on how their identities intersect within given contexts. Collins's (2000) scholarship on black feminist epistemologies has been instrumental in establishing the existence of a standpoint theory that centers subjugated knowledge within an intersectional framework. She explains:

> Each group speaks from its own standpoint and shares its own partial, situated knowledge. But because each group perceives its own truth as partial, its knowledge is unfinished. Each group becomes better able to consider other groups' standpoints without relinquishing the uniqueness of its own standpoint or suppressing other groups' partial perspectives. (p. 270)

It is worth noting, however, that Collins cautions against engaging in oppression comparisons when considering standpoint. Instead of comparing Black women's experiences with those of other minoritized groups, she emphasizes the importance of examining Black women's standpoint as one way among many to examine collective knowledge.

Future Considerations

Qualitative research grounded in critical frameworks provides access into the nuanced ways in which the glass ceiling works, as illuminated by the voices and counterstories of minoritized groups. More specifically, the interpretive frameworks of CRT and intersectionality can be important lenses through which glass ceiling research may be conducted as both offer critical standpoints that reveal gaps in current glass ceiling literature. As noted earlier, much of the current research tends to emphasize how White women experience glass ceiling effects. Applying a critical race perspective to guide qualitative research, then, grants scholars the ability to inquire into the role of White privilege in glass ceiling proliferation, asking, for example, how dominance, power, and entitlement intersect in the lives of those excluded by the glass ceiling. Additionally, researchers must challenge existing scholarly discourse through an intersectional lens; White female experiences cannot serve as the only standard through which the experiences of women

New Directions for Institutional Research • DOI: 10.1002/ir

of color should be examined. This approach simply reproduces essential-ist notions instead of challenging them, and as a result, the glass ceiling becomes a moving target for those wishing to advance in their careers.

Critically grounded qualitative studies are also needed to examine the policies, unspoken rules, and legal precedents that govern entry into em-ployment positions beyond the glass ceiling. These studies may be useful in understanding how individuals from minoritized groups navigate oppres-sive systems and carve out spaces that allow them to resist glass ceiling effects. For instance, among individuals who choose alternative career path-ways despite being positioned for advancement, what factors contribute to those decisions? Do they define success for themselves differently? How do individuals who advance beyond the glass ceiling navigate additional barriers they encounter at higher levels of employment in particular orga-nizations? Upon promotion, to what extent do they adopt the same hege-monic values that were initially used to prevent them from progressing up the employment ladder? Questions such as these lend themselves to crit-ical interpretivist lenses that consider glass ceiling effects from a range of perspectives. Such research still holds a wealth of promise to better capture the depth of experience for those disproportionately affected by the glass ceiling.

References

Bell, D. A. (1992). *Faces at the bottom of the well: The permanence of racism.* New York, NY: Basic Books.

Bell, D. A. (2000). Brown vs. Board of education: Forty-five years after the fact. *Ohio Northern Law Review, 26*(2), 171–182.

Bendl, R., & Schmidt, A. (2010). From 'Glass Ceilings' to 'Firewalls'—different metaphors for describing discrimination. *Gender, Work & Organization, 17*(5), 612–634.

Bogdan, R. C., & Biklen, S. K. (2006). *Qualitative research for education: An introduction to theories and methods* (5th ed.). Boston, MA: Allyn & Bacon.

Carnes, M., Morrissey, C., & Geller, S. E. (2008). Women's health and women's leader-ship in academic medicine: Hitting the same glass ceiling? *Journal of Women's Health, 17*(9), 1453–1462.

Collins, P. (2000). *Black feminist thought: Knowledge, consciousness, and the politics of empowerment* (2nd ed.). New York, NY: Routledge.

Cotter, D. A., Hermsen, J. M., Ovadia, S., & Vanneman, R. (2001). The glass ceiling effect. *Social Forces, 80*(2), 655–681.

Crenshaw, K. (1991). Mapping the margins: Intersectionality, identity politics, and vio-lence against women of color. *Stanford Law Review, 43*(6), 1241–1299.

Creswell, J. W. (2007). *Qualitative inquiry and research design: Choosing among five ap-proaches* (2nd ed.). Thousand Oaks, CA: Sage.

Delgado, R. (1995). *Critical race theory: The cutting edge.* Philadelphia, PA: Temple Uni-versity Press.

Delgado, R., & Stefancic, J. (2001). *Critical race theory: An introduction.* New York: New York University Press.

Elacqua, T. C., Beehr, T. A., Hansen, C. P., & Webster, J. (2009). Managers' beliefs about the glass ceiling: Interpersonal and organizational factors. *Psychology of Women Quarterly, 33*(3), 285–294.

Few, A. L. (2007). Integrating Black consciousness and critical race feminism into family studies research. *Journal of Family Issues, 28*(4), 452–473.

Forman, T. A. (2004). Color-blind racism and racial indifference: The role of racial apathy in facilitating enduring inequalities. In M. Krysan & A. E. Lewis (Eds.), *The changing terrain of race and ethnicity* (pp. 43–66). New York, NY: Russell Sage Foundation.

Harper, S. R., Patton, L. D., & Wooden, O. S. (2009). Access and equity for African American students in higher education: A critical race historical analysis of policy efforts. *The Journal of Higher Education, 80*(4), 389–414.

Harris, A. P. (1990). Race and essentialism in feminist legal theory. *Stanford Law Review, 42*(3), 581–616.

Hulko, W. (2009). The time- and context-contingent nature of intersectionality and interlocking oppressions. *Affilia, 24*(1), 44–55.

Jackson, J. F. L., & O'Callaghan, E. M. (2009). What do we know about glass ceiling effects? A taxonomy and critical review to inform higher education research. *Research in Higher Education, 50*(5), 460–482.

Ladson-Billings, G., & Tate, W. F., IV. (1995). Toward a critical race theory of education. *Teachers College Record, 97*(1), 47–68.

Livers, A., & Lewis, N. (2009). Breaking the concrete ceiling. *Black Enterprise, 39*(11), 56–57.

Merriam, S. B. (2002). *Qualitative research in practice: Examples for discussion and analysis.* San Francisco, CA: Jossey-Bass.

Mukherjee, A., Mukherjee, A., & Godard, B. (2006). Translating minoritized cultures: Issues of caste, class and gender. *Postcolonial Text, 2*(3), 1–23.

Solórzano, D. G., & Yosso, T. J. (2002). A critical race counterstory of race, racism and affirmative action. *Equity and Excellence in Education, 35*(2), 155–168.

Valdes, F., Culp, J. M., & Harris, A. P. (2002). Introduction: Battles waged, won, and lost: Critical race theory at the turn of the millennium. In F. Valdes, J. M. Culp, & A. P. Harris (Eds.), *Crossroads, directions, and a new critical race theory.* Philadelphia, PA: Temple University Press.

Lori D. Patton is an associate professor in the Higher Education and Student Affairs Program at the Indiana University–Purdue University Indianapolis.

Chayla M. Haynes is an assistant professor in the Higher Education and Student Affairs Program at the University of Northern Colorado.

3

This chapter reviews methodological issues surrounding the measurement of glass ceiling effects and summarizes findings from one cross-sectional analysis study.

Approximating Glass Ceiling Effects Using Cross-Sectional Data

Jerlando F. L. Jackson, Elizabeth M. O'Callaghan, Ryan P. Adserias

The literature on the glass ceiling is complex. As discussed in other chapters in this volume, some studies seek to validate its existence (Cotter, Hermsen, Ovadia, & Vanneman, 2001; Maume, 2004), while others seek to identify its cause (e.g., Powell & Butterfield, 1994). Still others estimate its effects (e.g., salary and position attainment disparities) or aim to unveil the experiences of women who have surmounted the glass ceiling (Davies-Netzley, 1998; Lyness & Thompson, 1997; Ragins, Townsend, & Mattis, 1998) or been held back by it (Morrison, White, & Von Velsor, 1987). Just three studies, however, have utilized the Cotter et al. (2001) model to measure for a glass ceiling—and thus separate the barrier from its cause and effects. These studies are most closely aligned with the research aims of the current chapter and are reviewed in-depth. Special focus is given to this small set of previous research for two reasons. First, it situates the current chapter within this existing research approach to identifying and measuring the existence of a glass ceiling. Second, these studies validate the proposition that the glass ceiling is separate from its effects; these studies clarify that the glass ceiling is a manifestation of patterns of discrimination at the workplace. The current chapter also seeks to do the same.

Cotter et al. (2001) contend that a full-scale investigation of the glass ceiling requires a longitudinal data set. However, the availability of such data for scholarly research—especially in regard to higher education—is limited. Longitudinal data, such as the Panel Study of Income Dynamics (PSID) and Census data, have been employed; however, locating longitudinal data relevant to specific industries or sectors of the economy can be extremely difficult. Does this mean that efforts to detect the glass ceiling, or its effects, should be abandoned? Not in the least. It does mean, however, that a modified approach to understanding the glass ceiling is required. This chapter illustrates how this may be done. Although it presents barriers to

NEW DIRECTIONS FOR INSTITUTIONAL RESEARCH, no. 159 © 2014 Wiley Periodicals, Inc.
Published online in Wiley Online Library (wileyonlinelibrary.com) • DOI: 10.1002/ir.20052

inference, analysis using cross-sectional data may offer valuable evidence toward substantiating claims that the glass ceiling exists. Although cross-sectional observational studies do not demonstrate changes over time, they do help to demonstrate the nature of gender or racial segregation at individual points in time. These findings when aggregated together may lead toward meaningful conclusions about how this particular form of discrimination occurs and perpetuates itself.

Full consideration of the underlying reasons why sex- and race-based discrimination exist in society is beyond the scope of the present chapter. Nevertheless, to briefly summarize, scholars (e.g., Ashraf, 1996; Bellas, 1993) have noted two primary explanations for the underrepresentation of women and people of color in particular industries and employment roles. Some have argued that the disparity is rooted in differing levels of human capital (i.e., education, training, and experience) which result in inequitable outcomes in salary and position attainment. In contrast, other scholars contend that sources of inequality go beyond the individual and arise from social and structural barriers that manifest in discriminatory hiring and promotion practices (Bellas, 1993; Jackson, 2006, 2008).

Beyond the debate above, the literature on the glass ceiling is vast and sometimes lacking in coherence. Indeed, the volume of journal articles and books on the subject indicate substantial scholarly interest, and many employment sectors have investigated the role of the glass ceiling in their own hiring and promotion programs. For example, the United States Federal Government (Powell & Butterfield, 1994; Yamagata, Yeh, Stewman, & Dodge, 1997), the United States military (Baldwin, 1996; Cohen, Broschak, & Haveman, 1998), major American corporations (Bartol, Martin, & Kromkowski, 2003; Bell, McLaughlin, & Sequeira, 2002; Morrison & Von Glinow, 1990; Morrison et al., 1987), and the higher education sector (Chliwniak, 1997; David & Woodward, 1997; Glazer-Raymo, 1999; Johnsrud, 1991) have all invested in research on the glass ceiling.

Notwithstanding the volume of research, there appears to be little agreement on what a glass ceiling actually is (Jackson & O'Callaghan, 2009). Numerous studies document the effects of the glass ceiling; however, many of these studies take its existence for granted, and neglect to first validate its existence from a quantitative perspective (Cotter et al., 2001). Before proceeding, two fundamental questions must be addressed: (a) what exactly is a glass ceiling? and (b) how do we know when one exists? Next we briefly discuss multiple studies that have attempted to answer each of these questions, interpreting and characterizing glass ceiling discrimination in varying manners. We then turn to reviewing literature on the effects of the glass ceiling in the specific case of female faculty where disparities are well documented, but attributing them to the glass ceiling remains methodologically fraught.

The Glass Ceiling

The glass ceiling is generally viewed as a set of impediments and/or barriers to career advancement for women and people of color (Baxter & Wright, 2000; Morrison & Von Glinow, 1990; Morrison et al., 1987). These impediments and/or barriers span a constellation of variables that often materialize into conscious and unconscious discriminatory practices (Lee, 2002; Martin, 1991, 1992; Padavic & Reskin, 2002; Ridgeway, 2001). As such, organizational policies and practices that disproportionately and negatively impact women and people of color effectively create a "hidden" system of discrimination (Morrison & Von Glinow, 1990). Therefore, the glass ceiling is typically acknowledged as a subtle, transparent barrier that prevents the advancement of women and people of color to the upper echelons of power and authority in the workforce (Cleveland, Stockdale, & Murphy, 2000; Morrison & Von Glinow, 1990). Additionally, the presence of a glass ceiling is often not explained by job-relevant qualifications of employees, or lack thereof. Rather, the glass ceiling may be a function of a multitude of forces: workplace social conditions, job requirements, and cultural biases (Cotter et al., 2001). Because of the glass ceiling's nebulous nature, often the only way to establish its existence is through an analysis of its effects.

Glass Ceiling Effects. Glass ceilings are revealed within an organization or industry vis-á-vis its effects. Some of the more traditional forms of discrimination that have been associated with a glass ceiling include disparities in job position (i.e., rank, authority, and title), salary, promotion potential, and level of responsibility as expressed through budgetary discretion and control (Ards, Brintnall, & Woodard, 1997; Athey, Avery, & Zemsky, 2000; Cotter, Hermsen, & Vanneman, 1999; Cotter et al., 2001; Ginther & Hayes, 1999; Landau, 1995). Scholars of higher education and other fields in academia have conducted studies of the glass ceiling and its effects on female faculty. Among these studies are examinations of law schools and legal education in business schools (Angel, 2000; Fisher, Motowidlo, & Werner, 1993); female economics faculty (Kahn, 1993); the humanities (Ginther & Hayes, 1999); the medical sciences (Carnes, Morrissey, & Geller, 2008; McGuire, Bergen, & Polan, 2004; Shea et al., 2011; Van den Brink, 2011); science, technology, engineering, and math fields (Liang & Bilimoria, 2007; Rosser, 1999, 2004); social work (Holley & Young, 2005); community colleges (Hagedorn & Laden, 2002); and international contexts (Bain & Cummings, 2000; Chesterman, Ross-Smith, & Peters, 2003; Van den Brink, 2011).

These interrogations of glass ceiling effects demonstrate that female faculty are more likely than male faculty to experience significant challenges advancing in their careers and were less likely to achieve the highest levels of recognition in their field (i.e., tenure). When pay disparities were examined, female faculty were also less likely to be compensated commensurate with their experience and career status. While these findings do not necessarily preclude the possibility that the differences resulted for reasons other than a glass ceiling, these outcomes are in line with existing theory on the phenomenon and its predicted effects.

Using Cross-Sectional Data to Understand Glass Ceiling Effects

While longitudinal data would offer a more definitive test of the glass ceiling in specific employment contexts, a preliminary analysis using cross-sectional data and multivariate analysis is helpful in determining whether further inquiry is warranted. For example, if statistically significant results are found to support a negative relationship between gender and opportunities for promotion when controlling for other related confounding factors, it would be prudent to locate longitudinal data to further investigate whether a pattern of statistically significant discrimination unfolds and intensifies over the course of a career—a basic description of the glass ceiling. So while cross-sectional data cannot offer definitive evidence of the existence of a glass ceiling, it can produce findings showing the strength of the relationship between known effects of a glass ceiling (i.e., lower salaries and less potential for promotion) and social characteristics (i.e., sex and race/ethnicity) holding constant other variables related to the accumulation of human capital (i.e., education and work experience).

It is possible to draw inferences about change over time while utilizing a cross-sectional design. Studies that do so typically examine different age groups (or groups with different experiences), and although observations occur at a single point in time, differences between the groups may be assessed using regression analysis. The use of regression analysis, which estimates the strength of the association between two variables, allows the researcher to infer the effects of age (or another independent variable) on a dependent variable (Ho, O'Farrell, Hong, & You, 2006).

One strength of this type of study is that it typically minimizes the time and cost associated with developmental studies. However, a statistically significant finding with respect to age (or growth or development) may not be attributable strictly speaking to those factors, but to unobservable characteristics related to cohort; individuals are a product of their experiences, and if not fully accounted for in the model, these alternate factors can induce spurious results. With cross-sectional research, there is no way to track individual-level human capital developmental trends, nor is there any way to determine whether results from these studies would mimic those from a longitudinal study of the same sample (Ho et al., 2006; Krathwohl, 1998).

Overview of Cross-Sectional and Longitudinal Data

Research employing cross-sectional analyses have come under increased scrutiny in recent years. Central to the critiques of the method are concerns over inflation of causal inference (CI) due to common method variance (CMV; Lindell & Brandt, 2000; Lindell & Whitney, 2001; Rind-fleisch, Malter, Ganesan, & Moorman, 2008). Podsakoff, MacKenzie, Lee, and Podsakoff (2003) define CMV as the spurious variance attributable to the measurement method rather the constructs the measures represent. Statistical methodologists point out designs constructed utilizing cross-sectional data collection regimes are prone to validity threats due to the use of one-shot, single rater, or single-source data (Lindell & Brandt, 2000). Remedies for avoiding such measurement and analytical errors include reliance on longitudinal data sets. Indeed, longitudinal data collection regimes are almost always preferable to one-shot data collection methods for the reasons described above; however, practical constraints in longitudinal data collection (i.e., time and money) typically inhibit research of critical importance, such as studies of glass ceiling effects.

Common Critiques of Cross-Sectional and Longitudinal Data. Statistical methodologists have identified several threats to validity associated with cross-sectional data collection and analysis techniques. Among these are errors associated with CMV, or spurious findings that result from measurement bias that may be correlated across variables and unaccounted for in the analysis. For example, survey questions in which respondents must choose a response category on a Likert or other common scale may be biased due to response effects across items (Rindfleisch et al., 2008). Further, survey respondents themselves may also induce systematic measurement error as scholars have shown that some respondents typically answer surveys in a consistent manner, or may be susceptible to fluctuating moods, influencing their response patterns based on the order in which the survey instrument is administered (Rindfleisch et al., 2008).

Typically, researchers suggest employing a longitudinal survey instrument to reduce the threats to CI posed by cross-sectional data, but longitudinal data may suffer from the very same problems of CMV and some additional drawbacks, as Rindfleisch and associates (2008) are careful to note. First, longitudinal studies are prone to considerable attrition problems, and where attrition occurs in a nonrandom fashion correlated with variables of interest, it poses a significant threat to the validity of inferences relying on these data. While panel data may be preferable to cross-sectional data in offering clearer evidence of temporal order, just as with cross-sectional analysis, CI with longitudinal data remains encumbered by the same caveats about unobserved omitted variables and measurement error (Granger, 1980).

Reducing the Risk of CMV on CI With Cross-Sectional Data. As scholars have come to recognize the impracticability of designing and implementing expensive longitudinal data collection regimes, some have offered various statistical means of accounting for, and correcting, threats to CI posed by CMV (see Lindell & Whitney, 2001). Among the recommendations suggested by researchers for reducing the risk of CMV bias include (a) collecting data from multiple respondents, (b) inclusion of multiple types of data sources, and (c) collecting data covering multiple time periods (Rind-fleisch et al., 2008). These suggestions, however, are not always feasible in the collection of data seeking to identify glass ceilings and their effects on academic workforces—most especially with regard to longitudinal collection. Inclusion of multiple types of data may also be unfeasible, hampered by similar time and financial constraints, and in some instances, access to, and use of, multiple forms of institutional data may be restricted by institutional policy.

In cases where longitudinal data collection may not be possible, cross-sectional data may still provide added clarity germane to issues concerning glass ceiling effects, or it may illuminate patterns warranting further investigation. Moreover, as literature suggests, cross-sectional data have been empirically shown, with careful planning of data collection regimes and under certain circumstances, not to produce the large CMV threats to CI as some scholars have feared. Indeed, as Rindfleisch and colleagues (2008) show, cross-sectional data may provide sufficient statistical power to make CI possible. Specifically, Rindfleisch et al. (2008) show that cross-sectional data may be appropriate under circumstances where "studies examine concrete and externally-oriented constructs, sample highly-educated [knowledgeable] respondents, employ a diverse array of measurement formats and scale, and are either descriptive in nature or strongly rooted in theory" (p. 274).

Many of these criteria can be satisfied for inquiry around glass ceiling effects for female administrators in institutions of higher education. Although the criterion recommending cross-sectional data be collected and analyzed primarily for external constructs is a means of reducing measurement error, careful research design that ensures anonymity of participants and their responses and takes steps to improve the accuracy of self-reporting can help reduce the risk of response biases, in particular those associated with socially undesirable or sensitive subjects (Gordon, 1987).

Studying Glass Ceiling Effects Using Cross-Sectional Data

The following section summarizes results from one study of glass ceiling effects, Jackson and O'Callaghan (2011). The study, "Understanding Employment Disparities Using Glass Ceiling Effects Criteria: An Examination of Race/Ethnicity and Senior-Level Position Attainment Across the Academic Workforce," focused on race and ethnicity as an independent predictor of employment. This study relied on cross-sectional data, specifically the 1999 cycle of the National Study of Postsecondary Faculty (NSOPF: 99), which is maintained by the National Center for Education Statistics (NCES). The study involved estimating logistic regression models with six separate dependent variables to identify the unique predictors of holding key academic positions. These included employment as teaching faculty (assistant professors, associated professors, and full professors) and employment in

Table 3.1. Summary of Findings in Jackson and O'Callaghan (2011)

	Finding	Outcome
Finding 1	People of color are less likely to hold entry-level faculty and administrative positions.	Compared to Whites, controlling for social and human capital, ability, motivation, and institutional characteristics, racial and ethnic minorities were least likely to hold entry-level faculty and administrative positions.
Finding 2	Perseverance past the entry level increases the likelihood of achieving senior-level faculty and administrative positions.	After advancement past the entry-level stages of a career, while holding position-appropriate social and human capital levels constant, as well as demonstrated ability, a high level of self-reported job satisfaction, and employment in the proper context, faculty and administrators of color are more likely than Whites to achieve senior-level career positions.
Finding 3	Effects of the glass ceiling may ameliorate over time.	Over time and with advancement, negative career outcomes for racial and ethnic minority faculty and administrators appear to diminish.
Finding 4	Institution type and fit play a significant role in career success and advancement.	Faculty and administrators of color employed at appropriately-fitted institutions experienced positive career success and professional advancement outcomes.

academic leadership positions (at the lower-level, mid-level, and upper-level).

Furthermore, the logistic regression models employed in the study include measures of social capital, human capital, ability, and motivation, and were designed to account for career progression through the ranks for of the academic workforce. The animating intent was to model, to the degree that is possible, important criteria and variables considered in both the hiring and promotion process—two important moments in which glass ceiling effects are expected to be apparent.

In effect, the models summarized here are designed to control for appropriate individual and institutional factors that may be correlated with both the independent variables of interest and the outcome variables, thus isolating a "theoretical situation" in which these other confounders remain fixed and only differences in the independent variable are modeled with all else equal. Therefore, when considering significant results by race/ethnicity, it is important to remember that they likely do not apply uniformly to everyone within that particular race/ethnic category, but rather approximate a general effect for those who have characteristics and attributes that align with the controls in these models.

While it is difficult for us to speak directly to the existence of the glass ceiling as the causal explanation behind observed employment differences by race/ethnicity, our findings provided new perspectives for understanding the nature of these disparities. Statistically significant results emerged for each of the models; however, the magnitude of these differences was small. Nonetheless, at least four conclusions based on the first two criteria from Cotter et al. (2001) for glass ceiling effects and about exclusionary practices may be drawn from the example study. These findings are reviewed in Table 3.1.

Conclusion

This example study offers claims about the effects of the glass ceiling. At times they were counterintuitive and contrary to basic theories of racial/ethnic discrimination in the workforce, but in other instances they confirm existing theories. We have summarized the findings here not as definitive evidence for the existence of the glass ceiling in academic hiring, but as examples of how analysis in causal-comparative research tradition can "examine relationships and make predictions in the presence of non-manipulated categorical variables" (Johnson, 2001, p. 6). By controlling for related confounding variables in a cross-sectional analysis, it is possible to make some modest inferences about causality, ruling out plausible alternative hypotheses explaining the disparities observed in the data.

The findings are compelling enough to warrant further investigation into the patterns of how glass ceiling effects emerge; however, cross-sectional analysis remains hindered by the barriers to CI discussed in this chapter, specifically cohort effects. For that reason, longitudinal data when possible to collect may help to clarify and explain the specific patterns of discrimination detected at any given cross-section in time. Both efforts of scholarly study help arm the research community with powerful evidence substantiating the overwhelming qualitative claims advanced that the glass ceiling exists and exerts considerable control over the work aspirations and opportunities for women and people of color in our society.

References

Angel, M. (2000). The glass ceiling for women in legal education: Contract positions and the death of tenure. *Journal of Legal Education, 50*, 1–15.

Ards, S., Brintnall, M., & Woodard, M. (1997). The road to tenure and beyond for African American political scientists. *The Journal of Negro Education, 66*(2), 159–171.

Ashraf, J. (1996). Is gender pay discrimination on the wane? Evidence from panel data, 1968–1989. *Industrial and Labor Relations Review, 49*(3), 537–546.

Athey, S., Avery, C., & Zemsky, P. (2000). Mentoring and diversity. *The American Economic Review, 90*(4), 765–786.

Bain, O., & Cummings, W. (2000). Academe's glass ceiling: Societal, professional/organizational, and institutional barriers to the career advancement of academic women. *Comparative Education Review, 44*(4), 493–514.

Baldwin, N. J. (1996). The promotion record of the United States Army: Glass ceilings in the Officer Corps. *Public Administration Review, 56*(2), 199–206.

Bartol, K. M., Martin, D. C., & Kromkowski, J. A. (2003). Leadership and the glass ceiling: Gender and ethnic group influences on leader behaviors at middle and executive managerial levels. *Journal of Leadership & Organizational Studies, 9*(3), 8–20.

Baxter, J., & Wright, E. O. (2000). The glass ceiling hypothesis: A comparative study of the United States, Sweden, and Australia. *Gender and Society, 14*(2), 275–294.

Bell, M. P., McLaughlin, M. E., & Sequeira, J. M. (2002). Discrimination, harassment and the glass ceiling: Women executives as change agents. *Journal of Business Ethics, 37*(1), 65–76.

Bellas, M. (1993). Faculty salaries: Still a cost of being female? *Social Science Quarterly, 74*(1), 62–75.

Carnes, M., Morrissey, C., & Geller, S. E. (2008). Women's health and women's leadership in academic medicine: Hitting the same glass ceiling? *Journal of Women's Health, 17*(9), 1453–1462.

Chesterman, C., Ross-Smith, A., & Peters, M. (2003). Changing the landscape? Women in academic leadership in Australia. *McGill Journal of Education, 38*(3), 421–436.

Chliwniak, L. (1997). *Higher education leadership: Analyzing the gender gap* [ASHE-ERIC Higher Education Reports, 25(4), 1–97]. Washington, DC: Graduate School of Education and Human Development, The George Washington University.

Cleveland, J. N., Stockdale, M., & Murphy, K. R. (2000). *Women and men in organizations: Sex and gender issues at work.* Mahwah, NJ: Erlbaum.

Cohen, L. E., Broschak, J. P., & Haveman, H. A. (1998). And then there were more? The effect of organizational sex composition on the hiring and promotion of managers. *American Sociological Review, 63*(5), 711–727.

Cotter, D. A., Hermsen, J. M., Ovadia, S., & Vanneman, R. (2001). The glass ceiling effect. *Social Forces, 80*(2), 655–682.

Cotter, D. A., Hermsen, J. M., & Vanneman, R. (1999). Systems of gender, race, and class inequality: Multilevel analyses. *Social Forces, 78*(2), 433–460.

David, M., & Woodward, D. (Eds.). (1997). *Negotiating the glass ceiling—Careers of senior women in the academic world.* Washington, DC: Falmer Press.

Davies-Netzley, S. A. (1998). Women above the glass ceiling: Perceptions on corporate mobility and strategies for success. *Gender and Society, 12*(3), 339–355.

Fisher, B. D., Motowidlo, S., & Werner, S. (1993). Effects of gender and other factors on rank of law professors in colleges of business: Evidence of a glass ceiling. *Journal of Business Ethics, 12*(10), 771–778.

Ginther, D. K., & Hayes, K. J. (1999). Gender differences in salary and promotion in the humanities. *The American Economic Review, 89*(2), 397–402.

Glazer-Raymo, J. (1999). *Shattering the myths: Women in academe.* Washington, DC: Johns Hopkins Press.

Gordon, R. A. (1987). Social desirability bias: A demonstration and technique for its reduction. *Teaching of Psychology, 14*(1), 40–42.

Granger, C. W. J. (1980). Testing for causality: A personal viewpoint. *Journal of Economic Dynamics and Control, 2*, 329–352.

Hagedorn, L. S., & Laden, B. V. (2002). Exploring the climate for women as community college faculty. In C. L. Outcalt (Ed.), *New Directions for Community College: No. 118. Community college faculty: Characteristics, practices, and challenges* (pp. 69–78). San Francisco, CA: Jossey Bass.

Ho, H., O'Farrell, S. L., Hong, S., & You, S. (2006). Developmental research: Theory, method, design and statistical analysis. In J. L. Green, G. Camilli, & P. B. Elmore (Eds.), *Handbook of complementary methods in education research* (pp. 207–226). Mahwah, NJ: Lawrence Erlbaum.

Holley, L. C., & Young, D. S. (2005). Career decisions and experiences of social work faculty: A gender comparison. *Journal of Social Work Education, 41*(2), 297–313.

Jackson, J. F. L. (2006). Hiring practices of African American males in academic leadership position at American colleges and universities: An employment trends and disparate impact analysis. *Teachers College Record, 108*(2), 316–338.

Jackson, J. F. L. (2008). Race segregation across the academic workforce: Exploring factors that may contribute to the disparate representation of African American men. *American Behavioral Scientist, 51*, 1004–1029.

Jackson, J. F. L., & O'Callaghan, E. M. (2009).What do we know about glass ceiling effects? A taxonomy and critical review to inform higher education research. *Research in Higher Education, 50*(5), 460–482.

Jackson, J. F. L., & O'Callaghan, E. M. (2011). Understanding employment disparities using glass ceiling effects criteria: An examination of race/ethnicity and senior-level position attainment across the academic workforce. *Journal of the Professoriate, 5*(2), 67–99.

Johnson, B. (2001). Toward a new classification of nonexperimental quantitative research. *Educational Researcher, 30*(2), 3–13.

Johnsrud, L. K. (1991). Administrative promotion: The power of gender. *The Journal of Higher Education, 62*(2), 119–149.

Kahn, S. (1993). Gender differences in academic career paths of economists. *The American Economic Review, 83*(2), 52–56.

Krathwohl, D. R. (1998). *Methods of educational and social science research, an integrated approach* (2nd ed.). Long Grove, IL: Waveland Press.

Landau, J. (1995). The relationship of race and gender to managers' ratings of promotion potential. *Journal of Organizational Behavior, 16*(4), 391–400.

Lee, S. M. (2002). Do Asian American faculty face a glass ceiling? *American Educational Research Journal, 39*(3), 695–724.

Liang, X., & Bilimoria, D. (2007). The representation and experience of women faculty in STEM fields. In R. J. Burke & M. C. Mattis (Eds.), *Women and minorities in science, technology, engineering and mathematics: Upping the numbers* (pp. 317–333). Northampton, MA: Edward Elgar.

Lindell, M. K., & Brandt, C. J. (2000). Climate quality and climate consensus as mediators of the relationship between organizational antecedents and outcomes. *Journal of Applied Psychology, 85*(3), 331–348.

Lindell, M. K., & Whitney, D. J. (2001). Accounting for common method variance in cross-sectional research designs. *Journal of Applied Psychology, 86*(1), 114–121.

Lyness, K. S., & Thompson, D. E. (1997). Above the glass ceiling? A comparison of matched samples of female and male executives. *Journal of Applied Psychology, 82*(3), 359–375.

Martin, L. (1991). *A report on the glass ceiling commission.* Washington, DC: U.S. Department of Labor.

Martin, L. (1992). *Pipelines of progress—A status report on the glass ceiling.* Washington, DC: U.S. Department of Labor.

Maume, D. J., Jr. (2004). Is the glass ceiling a unique form of inequality? Evidence from a random-effects model of managerial attainment. *Work and Occupations, 31*(2), 250–274.

McGuire, L. K., Bergen, M. R., & Polan, M. L. (2004). Career advancement for women faculty in a US school of medicine: Perceived needs. *Academic Medicine, 79*(4), 319–325.

Morrison, A. M., & Von Glinow, M. A. (1990). Women and minorities in management. *American Psychologist*, 45(2), 200–208.

Morrison, A. M., White, R. P., & Von Velsor, E. (1987). *Breaking the glass ceiling: Can women reach the top of America's largest corporations?* Reading, MA: Addison-Wesley.

Padavic, I., & Reskin, B. (2002). *Men and women at work.* Thousand Oaks, CA: Pine Forge Press.

Podsakoff, P. M., MacKenzie, S. B., Lee, J.-Y., & Podsakoff, N. P. (2003). Common method biases in behavioral research: A critical review of the literature and recommended remedies. *Journal of Applied Psychology*, 88(5), 879–903.

Powell, G. N., & Butterfield, D. A. (1994). Investigating the "glass ceiling" phenomenon: An empirical study of actual promotions to top management. *The Academy of Management Journal*, 37(1), 68–86.

Ragins, B. R, Townsend, B., & Mattis, M. (1998). Gender gap in the executive suite: CEOs and female executives report on breaking the glass ceiling. *The Academy of Management Executive*, 12(1), 28–42.

Ridgeway, C. L. (2001). Gender, status and leadership. *Journal of Social Issues*, 57(4), 637–655.

Rindfleisch, A., Malter, A. J., Ganesan, S., & Moorman, C. (2008). Cross-sectional versus longitudinal survey research: Concepts, findings, and guidelines. *Journal of Marketing Research*, 45(3), 261–279.

Rosser, S. V. (1999). Different laboratory/work climates: Impacts on women in the workplace. *Annals of the New York Academy of Sciences*, 869(1), 95–101.

Rosser, S. V. (2004). *The science glass ceiling: Academic women scientists and the struggle to succeed.* New York, NY: Psychology Press.

Shea, J. A., Stern, D. T., Klotman, P. E., Clayton, C. P., O'Hara, J. L., Feldman, M. D., ... Jagsi, R. (2011). Career development of physician scientists: A survey of leaders in academic medicine. *The American Journal of Medicine*, 124(8), 779–787.

Van den Brink, M. (2011). Scouting for talent: Appointment practices of women professors in academic medicine. *Social Science & Medicine*, 72(12), 2033–2040.

Yamagata, H., Yeh, K. S., Stewman, S., & Dodge, H. (1997). Sex segregation and glass ceilings: A comparative statics model of women's career opportunities in the federal government over a quarter century. *The American Journal of Sociology*, 103(3), 566–632.

JERLANDO F. L. JACKSON is the Vilas Distinguished Professor of higher education, and director and chief research scientist for Wisconsin's Equity and Inclusion Laboratory (Wei LAB) at the University of Wisconsin-Madison.

ELIZABETH M. O'CALLAGHAN is a lecturer in the Department of Educational Leadership and Policy Analysis at the University of Wisconsin-Madison.

RYAN P. ADSERIAS is a research associate for Wisconsin's Equity and Inclusion Laboratory (Wei LAB) and a doctoral student at the University of Wisconsin-Madison in educational leadership and policy analysis.

This chapter explores eliminating faculty-related glass ceiling effects through academic governance.

Faculty Diversity and the Traditions of Academic Governance

James T. Minor

The task of running a university now entails managing multimillion dollar budgets, navigating legal intricacies, orchestrating extensive fundraising activities, and, in some cases, directing auxiliaries, such as university medical centers or large-scale collegiate athletic programs. Over the last two decades, institutions of higher education saw a 51% increase in full-time administrators (McCurtis, Jackson, & O'Callaghan, 2009). During this same period, serious questions emerged concerning declining faculty involvement in campus decision making (Burgan, 1998; Collie & Chronister, 2001; Minor, 2004). Nevertheless, the changing nature of faculty work, their orientation toward leadership, and their increasingly diverse career paths have important implications for future leadership in the academy (Baldwin, Lunceford, & Vanderlinden, 2005).

More recently, scholars have given greater attention not only to how faculty careers develop but also which individuals' careers are progressing with respect to racial or gender differences (Cooper & Stevens, 2002; Lee, 2002; Tierney & Sallee, 2008). In the last decade, for instance, there has been significant discussion concerning the ascension of a small number of women presidents at prestigious higher education institutions. Simultaneously, higher education has been confronted with an aging professoriate and a gross underrepresentation of women and minorities, especially in STEM-related fields (Gappa, Austin, & Trice, 2007). In the last 30 years, universities have implemented institutional diversity plans, hired chief diversity officers, and endured legal battles in the name of increasing campus diversity (Iverson, 2007).

Although there have been gains in some areas, diversifying faculty has proven most difficult. From 1996 to 2006, minority students experienced a 63% increase in the number of bachelor's degrees earned, which compared to an improvement of 24% among Whites. Latina women made the most significant gains, experiencing a 97% increase in bachelor's degrees earned

NEW DIRECTIONS FOR INSTITUTIONAL RESEARCH, no. 159 © 2014 Wiley Periodicals, Inc.
Published online in Wiley Online Library (wileyonlinelibrary.com) • DOI: 10.1002/ir.20053

over the same 10-year period (Ryu, 2008). Additionally, from 1983 to 2003, higher education experienced a 200% increase in the number of full-time minority administrators (McCurtis et al., 2009), yet African Americans constitute fewer than 3% of all full professors compared to 2% for Latinos, 6% for Asians, and 88% for Whites (Ryu, 2008). Similar disparities exist among the ranks of associate and assistant professors. This demographic imbalance among faculty is of critical importance given that the majority of executive administrators, such as presidents, provosts, and deans, still ascend from tenured faculty positions in higher education. Consequently, the same disparities in faculty ranks are visible among senior-level administrators in higher education.

Glass ceiling effects are generally defined as attitudinal or organizational biases that prevent minorities and women from advancing to leadership positions (Bain & Cummings, 2000). I argue that glass ceiling effects and the lack of career progression among faculty of color are better understood by examining the traditions of academic governance.

Matters of faculty diversity and career progression persist in a context that limits the involvement of central administrators due to high levels of professional autonomy. Most studies that address racial and ethnic diversity among faculty do so from a perspective that promotes virtues of multiculturalism and inclusion yet ignore the systems and procedures that impact how decisions are actually made in the academy. This chapter balances arguments for eliminating faculty-related glass ceiling effects with characteristics of academic governance. Doing so provides institutional leaders with a better perspective on opportunities to reduce structural and cultural barriers within institutions. This approach helps identify institutional policies that obstruct goals to diversify faculty composition, and ultimately, senior administrators as well. I bring together principles of faculty diversity and academic governance to highlight conceptual incongruence that impedes progress.

Refocusing the Conceptual Frame

Equally important to demonstrating disparities in the higher education workforce is understanding why they exist and how to address them effectively. Beyond complying with federal anti-discrimination laws, colleges and universities struggle to create and sustain environments that feature rich faculty diversity. This, of course, produces negative consequences for diversifying the composition of senior-level academic administrators. Despite committed rhetoric and significant investments in programs aimed to improve campus climate, faculty hiring and promotion practices remain fundamentally unchanged. As such, future discussions about glass ceiling effects in higher education require a better understanding of two fundamental concepts inherent in colleges and universities: academic freedom and structural looseness.

NEW DIRECTIONS FOR INSTITUTIONAL RESEARCH • DOI: 10.1002/ir

These conceptual frames are necessary complements to empirical studies that analyze glass ceiling effects and administrative strategies aimed at improving workforce equity in higher education. This chapter, therefore, addresses both concepts in relation to faculty promotion and tenure, both critical career milestones related to faculty retention and access to executive positions in higher education. Accurate conceptual frames are a necessary complement to empirical studies that analyze glass ceiling effects and administrative strategies aimed at improving workforce equity in higher education.

Faculty Diversity in Higher Education

Glass ceiling effects and the lack of faculty diversity are often described as "pipeline" issues related to insufficient numbers of minorities earning graduate degrees to fill positions. Although the concept has some merit it does not entirely account for disparities in faculty rank, especially among women. These disparities exist not only horizontally—as demonstrated through the overall number of minorities who hold faculty rank—but also vertically, or the disproportionately low number of women and minority faculty with tenure or full professor status. According to recent data from the U.S. Department of Education, about 91% of full professors at research universities are White and 75% are male. Only 5% of full professors in the nation are African American, Latino, or Native American. Additionally, half of all African American faculty in the country are employed at Historically Black Colleges and Universities (HBCUs). Moreover, the proportion of African American faculty at predominately White institutions, 2.3%, is practically the same as it was 30 years ago (Knapp, Kelly-Reid, & Ginder, 2008).

Given the fact that women now earn more than half of all awarded master's degrees and 44% of awarded doctorate degrees (Trower & Chait, 2002), it follows then that so-called pipeline issues do not provide an adequate, comprehensive explanation for these data. Female faculty are also more likely to hold lower academic ranks and work at less-prestigious institutions even though the proportion of men doing so has significantly decreased over the last two decades (Snyder, Dillow, & Hoffman, 2009).

Organizational structures and cultural traditions also warrant some consideration. Examining such factors will likely help institutional leaders better understand why academia is so immune to initiatives aimed at improving faculty diversity and career progression. This lack of progress is attributable not only to social forces, leadership, or policy but also organizational characteristics. Institutions of higher education traditionally maintain high levels of autonomy that buffer them, structurally and culturally, from external, and in some cases internal, forces. These behaviors have long been the subject of study in higher education (Ikenberry, 1971; Mortimer, 1971; Pfnister, 1970) and for more than 30 years, scholars have theorized about how universities work. Most agree that colleges—as organizations—operate in a distinctly different manner than any other social institution. As a result, any typical understanding of glass ceiling effects or workplace equity gleaned from the business community, for example, do not necessarily translate to university settings.

Karl Weick (1976) established the notion that, unlike most other social organizations, universities are characterized by ambiguous goals, mismatches in technology, and highly autonomous professional cores. Colleges and universities promote far-reaching mission statements, such as "transforming lives," "advancing knowledge," or "promoting diverse learning environments," but these goals are usually plagued by ambiguous interpretation and pursued through disparate channels that are only tenuously linked to the institution's mission statement or goals. Additionally, the means or technologies by which these ambiguous goals are accomplished are not always clear. For example, a university president might wish to improve campus climate by making the university community more tolerant of differences, but the means to achieve such a goal are typically imprecise and, in some cases, disagreeable. Campus leaders might hold sensitivity training for staff, create space for marginalized students, or offer a one-credit seminar to first-year students. Rarely have these practices, which vary in execution, been subject to empirical testing, and there is typically little evidence demonstrating their relative effectiveness. In addition to disparate and sometimes contradicting institutional activity, the professional core—faculty—enjoy an exceptionally high level of autonomy to define, conduct, and evaluate their work. I discuss two institutional hallmarks that also potentially obstruct efforts to improve faculty diversity and career advancement.

Academic Freedom

Academic freedom, according to the American Association of University Professors' (AAUP) 1940 statement, refers to the notion that faculty ought to possess the freedom to teach, research, and publish without interference of university administrators or external pressures. The AAUP articulated the concept of academic freedom in the early 1900s and it has withstood the test of time and the U.S. legal system to become a foundational attribute of higher education. Faculty, across disciplinary lines, should be free to follow the paths of truth wherever they may lead. The principles of academic freedom are not absolute, however; special obligations to speak and teach with appropriate restraint and responsibility to institutional affiliations are generally recognized.

Still, faculty enjoy an exceptionally high degree of autonomy in defining and conducting their work. In the years following the AAUP statement, tenure policies and faculty ranking systems served as mechanisms to insulate academic freedom, although many scholars continue to question the value of tenure and the process by which it is awarded. Some, for example, argue that the system is broken and that tenure itself has become the goal rather the means to preserve academic freedom (Chait, 2002; Tierney, 2004). Tabling this debate about the place of tenure in the academy, the remainder of this chapter focuses on one less-discussed consequence of academic freedom: decision making.

The principles of academic freedom and autonomy typically grant faculty influence, in theory and practice, over teaching and learning. Faculty reserve the right to make decisions about which collections of courses merit degrees, the sequences in which courses are offered, and which materials are used to deliver content. Faculty, within the tenure system, also reserve the right to evaluate the merits of their colleagues. University administrators have traditionally deferred to faculty when determining what educational experiences are required to train future professionals across various disciplines. But of all decision-making domains, faculty exercise the most authority over areas traditionally considered their purview, namely curriculum development, the quality of academic programs, and the evaluation of teaching (Tierney & Minor, 2003). Faculty also resist the intrusion of administrators in matters of training electrical engineers or third-grade math teachers, asserting the right to evaluate the merits of their colleagues' disciplinary contributions through their teaching, research, and service (Chait, 2002).

Apart from the initiatives advanced by the chief diversity officer or the latest speech from the president about multiculturalism, senior faculty—in large part—determine who is hired or awarded tenure. In many cases, these decisions are made with little attention to institutions' diversity efforts, and with few, if any, consequences for failing to do so. Ideally, tenure and promotion decisions are based on (albeit subjective) assessments of individuals' professional merits in relation to disciplinary standards and institutional guidelines. There is also mounting evidence, however, that suggests tenure entails a sociopolitical component as well—one that disadvantages minority candidates (Tierney & Bensimon, 1996; Turner & Myers, 1999). To be clear, a fundamental overhaul of the tenure process may not be the answer; these observations are offered only in an effort to draw attention to the question of the effectiveness of central diversity policies and/or other campus-wide initiatives aimed at improving faculty diversity. While efforts to improve faculty diversity or the retention of minority professors eligible for administrative positions weigh heavily on senior administrators, these endeavors are ultimately under the purview of the faculty.

Although universities are dynamic social environments in which no single variable directly influences outcomes, faculty autonomy in decision making has been an underexplored topic with respect to faculty diversity, especially as it relates to academic freedom (Eckel, 2006). Most university administrators are rightfully cautious not to dictate the terms of faculty appointments or evaluations, treating such intrusions as a violation of faculty autonomy (Kouzes & Posner, 2003). Administrators, often in collaboration with faculty, establish policies intended to guide hiring and promotion practices to ensure quality. Diversity is often considered a favorable by-product of faculty decision making. But even where faculty diversity is a goal promoted at the highest ranks of university administrations, there tend to be few, if any, consequences levied upon a committee of tenured full professors who disregard it in their decision making. In academia, few would argue that diversity interests should trump quality; the two would ideally coexist. Still, faculty, as critical decision makers, must willingly internalize the mission of increasing diversity, an oft-overlooked component of achieving institutional success.

Achieving faculty and administrative diversity is typically considered a central institutional goal, yet one of the most important hurdles—tenure and promotion of minority faculty—is determined locally with very little administrative influence or goal reinforcement. Additionally, current data regarding the distribution of faculty by rank and race indicate very little minority representation among those full professors actually making the hiring and promotion decisions (Knapp et al., 2008). Leaders interested in eliminating glass ceiling effects must instead account for those institutional characteristics that might obstruct central administrative efforts to remedy such discriminatory practices. The notion that administrators can achieve these goals simply by virtue of promoting diversity agendas is a fallacy when considered in the context of traditions of academic freedom, professional autonomy, and academic decision making. Decision-making authority remains situated in an environment that buffers faculty from administrative influence, with little external pressure to address these disparities or modify governance practices. Accordingly, improving faculty diversity remains the responsibility of mostly middle-aged, White males who suffer no consequences for maintaining the status quo.

Structural Looseness

The organizing principle of decentralization in higher education consists of various units within a university working to achieve fundamental goals while operating in distinct disciplinary silos with only minimal levels of responsiveness (Weick, 1976). Mathematics faculty, for example, may have little knowledge of or interest in programs offered in Spanish, yet these autonomous units are bound together by the institution's overarching mission. Institutions of higher education are characterized as loosely coupled given this tradition of disciplinary silos. One organizational benefit of loosely coupled systems is that individual units are buffered from failure in other units (Orton & Weick, 1990); a university might have a nationally recognized program in one college and another program on the brink of closure in a different college without any negative cross-effects. Additionally, universities can isolate problem areas while promoting institutional success in other areas. Potential drawbacks of such systems include the duplication of efforts, inefficiency, and communication problems that serve to limit opportunities for sensible collaboration (Weick, 1976).

Because universities are complex organizations, they are not necessarily subject to standardized policies or practices. As a result, institutional activities and outcomes are variable and unpredictable. Earning a nursing degree might require practicum rotations in local hospitals, psychology students might conduct evaluations of children, and studio art programs might have their students collaborate with international galleries. Each program is guided or restricted by different institutional policies or procedures that do not necessarily intersect. Likewise, policies that make sense for governing one unit of a university might conflict with another—as in the case for cultural differences across disciplines that guide disparate faculty work and decision-making processes (Birnbaum, 1988). Faculty in the Department of Fishery and Wildlife might be expected to conduct outreach to local agricultural communities. Faculty in the Department of Teacher Education might be expected to provide professional development activities for local teachers, whereas political scientists or historians may never be expected to conduct outreach. The range of university activity demands flexible polices and a sufficient degree of structural looseness to operate effectively.

This lack of structural regulation also influences decision making associated with faculty personnel assessments. In the same vein, evaluating merit in a respective unit and determining the metrics used to appraise it are equally context-specific. The extent of structural looseness not only applies to various units across a university but also within them. Different departments within a particular college might apply varied methods to evaluate a candidate for tenure or promotion. The methods and metrics used for assessment might also vary from one candidate to the next within the same department. While loose coupling in universities is more often discussed as an enabling feature rather than an obstacle, the system invites subjectivity based on faculty perspectives that limits regularity or the influence of administrative priorities. To be clear, institutions need not do away with faculty governance in favor of heavy-handed administrative interference. Instead, I simply call attention to these organizational features of universities in that they may hinder the effects of top-down policies aimed at improving diversity and retention. Scholars have favorably characterized academic freedom and organizational autonomy as core elements of academia, but they have yet to consider these concepts in relation to diversity efforts (Gumport, 2001).

Disciplinary subjectivity concerning tenure and promotion decisions limits administrative responses save for cases of clear violations of university policies or the law. Given the structural looseness of universities and the absence of specific criteria for awarding tenure, administrators are rarely in positions to question faculty decision making in relation to diversity agendas, limiting the extent to which the tenure process may be subject to increased regulation (Gappa et al., 2007). The structure of academic units, the nature of faculty work, what constitutes merit, and how it is assessed all vary considerably across and within institutions. As a result, it is difficult to prescribe central policies or institutional practices that might redress glass ceiling effects. Although some institutions use personnel committees at the university level to balance local tendencies while ensuring institutional quality, this practice has been met with a lukewarm reception because it narrows the definition of merit. Additionally, colleagues across disciplines have become less able to distinguish the nuances of faculty work relative to their departmental needs or those of their fields of study.

Aligning Ideas, Goals, and Action

College and university administrators have tended to promote the principle of faculty diversity without exercising direct influence over how faculty are actually hired, tenured, or promoted. Skeptics call diversity plans and associated polices "window dressing" given the real and perceived lack of progress. One might argue that a lack of progress is a clear indication that university leaders are either disingenuous or have yet to devise institutional strategies that effectively improve faculty diversity. I do not necessarily believe the former. Instead, most have not considered the fact that diversity goals, institutional policies, and academic culture are often asynchronous. To elaborate, 30 years of diversity work has taught us two important lessons. First, institutional "diversity plans" are relatively ineffective. Iverson (2007) argues that these plans actually perpetuate diversity-related problems by treating minorities with discursive framing that positions them as outsiders, victims, and commodities. In the early 1990s, for instance, scores of institutions announced campus-wide diversity plans that aimed to achieve certain percentages of minority representation across various categories over a 10-year period, but the majority of institutions failed to achieve their stated goals, and these plans soon fell out of favor. The second lesson reveals that universities have developed a healthy immunity to faculty diversity as conceived by its proponents. That is, simply promoting the virtue of diversity as an institutional value is ineffective, even with the presence of incentives.

If institutions of higher education are to improve the representation of minority faculty and retain them long enough to pursue administrative positions, campus leaders must more clearly recognize why previous efforts have been ineffectual. Polices and action must be more carefully tailored to the decision-making culture of colleges and universities. Certainly, no single policy or action will suit every campus but a conceptually different approach might. Rather than centrally promoting the goal of faculty diversity, campus leaders must make promoting faculty diversity more locally relevant.

Faculty Searches.   Faculty hiring represents a critical stage that invariably influences institutions' success at improving faculty diversity among minorities, especially in research-intensive universities where such individuals are least likely to land tenure-track positions (Cooper & Stevens, 2002; Knapp et al., 2008). Academic traditions dictate that a small committee tends to identify and evaluate the merit of potential colleagues relative to the needs of a particular department. Most faculty searches are bound by institutional criteria and protocol that aim to ensure equal opportunity treatment of applicants. Yet institutions have not gone so far as to ensure actual observation of these policies. Beyond compliance reporting, little is known about the actual execution of faculty hiring processes.

The challenges associated with committee composition is also worthy of consideration given the demographic representation of tenured faculty—a prerequisite to serve or vote on many personnel committees. A recent study of 689 faculty searches across three large public research institutions revealed that "almost all search committees were entirely White" (Smith, Turner, Osei-Kofi, & Richards, 2004, p. 154). Compounding this challenge is the notion of sponsorship—that is, when a senior committee member formally or informally recommends or promotes an individual as his or her candidate of choice for a particular position (Johnsrud, 1991). Even in the rare instances when there is minority representation on committees, the practice of sponsorship can undermine the integrity of these search processes. Committee composition, then, represents another critical point in the process in which data may be gathered to enable administrators to engage various units about their practices relative to broader institutional goals.

The notion of administrative intervention does not necessarily require that faculty relinquish their right to identify or select potential colleagues. Neither does it suggest that faculty are untrustworthy. I advocate for a stronger, more mutually beneficial working relationship between faculty and administrators. There are instances where administrative interventions have assisted in improving faculty diversity without sacrificing autonomy. For instance, administrative incentives that encourage deans and departments to recruit minority faculty more aggressively by providing financial support for new positions—commonly known as opportunity hires—have been effective strategies in diversifying applicant pools (Smith et al., 2004). The administrative involvement discussed here pertains to cooperative rather than intrusive processes that more tightly couple institutional goals with practice.

In another example, some campuses have gone so far as to mandate that outside faculty members, highly respected full professors from different colleges, participate as nonvoting members of faculty search committees in the hopes that they do so without personal investment, merely to observe the deliberations. At the end of the process, outside members complete short reports that describe the composition of the committee, the integrity of the process in accordance with university guidelines, and general impressions about the search processes relative to institutional priorities or stated position descriptions. The chief academic administrator then reviews the reports and aggregates them with others. While this single measure does not completely remedy the aforementioned challenges, it does help reduce the insular perspectives with which committees often go about their work. The ideas discussed above are not designed to give "preferential treatment" to any candidate. Instead, they are suggested as methods of better aligning institutional goals more closely with practice. Diversity models in higher education still assume that minority candidates are less qualified or less common, thereby requiring special treatment. As such, the problem is perceived to exist outside the institution. Rarely do higher education diversity models portray an institution, its structure, and its culture as contributing factors to any lack of progress. Alternatively, appropriate faculty search methods ought to take into account institutional practices, striving to reduce glass ceiling effects by minimizing obstacles that inadvertently prevent the hiring and promoting of minority faculty.

Tenure and Promotion.   The awarding of tenure and promotion to full professor are two important career milestones typically required before minority faculty qualify for senior administrative positions. In a national study of postsecondary faculty, women received lower salaries than their male counterparts, had lower probabilities of being tenured, and were less likely than men to be full professors, after controlling for experience, education, productivity, and institutional characteristics (Chernesky, 2003). Qualified minority faculty were also less likely to receive tenure, to be promoted to full professor, or to move into administrative positions (Jackson, 2008; Johnsrud & Heck, 1994). Similarly, Hispanic and Black faculty were also less likely than Whites to be tenured or promoted to full professor in four-year institutions, even when they were found to be more productive in certain cases (Perna, 2001). Although scholars continue to debate the merits of tenure, there is consensus that in practice it remains imperfect (Chait, 2002; O'Meara, 2004).

The opportunity to improve representation of women and minority leadership on decision-making committees has critical consequences beyond mere tokenism. Because so few minority faculty lead personnel committees, those who do so are in turn encumbered with an undue burden. Policies that prohibit lower-ranking faculty from voting during personnel deliberations are worthy of reassessment. Since both women and minorities are less likely to hold tenured positions or full professor positions, the resulting imbalance may sometimes be self-perpetuating, giving rise to static decision-making environments. Policies that prohibit lower-ranking voting privileges also increase the difficulty of forming committees that are truly representative of the population of evaluated individuals. In the presence of clear institutional and disciplinary criteria for awarding tenure or elevating scholars to full professor, faculty at any rank should be capable of making informed, judicious, well-reasoned decisions. The notion that one must be a full professor to judge materials concerning promotion, for example, is unfounded. The status-based right to participate in these committees contradicts ideals of shared governance and collegiality—principles often considered emblematic of higher education. Instead, institutions would be better served by legislating greater representation on personnel committees rather than relying on rank as the primary basis for committee formation. Given disparities among faculty levels, the probability of underrepresentation on committees is obvious. Such changes will likely go a long way toward ensuring more balanced assessments of faculty work and more judicious deliberations about the value of promoting faculty members.

Enacting such changes certainly does not perfect the faculty tenure and promotion processes. Even when junior faculty are represented, they can be silenced during decision-making processes. Even well-intentioned dissenters are often fearful of retribution or rebuke that may negatively influence their chances of being promoted (Cooper & Stevens, 2002). Effectual collegial decision-making in universities also requires vigorous debate. Consequently, institutions must focus attention on finding systematic ways of establishing feedback channels that give voice to alternative viewpoints while protecting individuals moving through the ranks. Some institutions, for example, allow for the submission of two documents from a forwarding committee to provide a platform for minority voting opinions during tenure and promotion deliberations. In instances when consensus is not reached, senior members of tenure and promotion committees submit both documents and deliberations are more fully represented.

Conclusion

Higher education scholarship does not typically treat concepts such as academic freedom and faculty diversity as potentially in conflict with one another. Advocates of academic freedom rarely claim to be opponents of faculty diversity. But there exists a tension, perhaps best described as a delicate equilibrium, between these two concepts that might more accurately explain the relationship between faculty diversity and academic governance.

Faculty diversity is a long-standing challenge for higher education institutions. While leaky pipelines and career choices among minority candidates are among the external explanations offered for the lack of progress, the role of internal factors in contributing to this result remains less clear. Critical race theorists might argue that institutions are inherently racist environments where discriminatory views and practices produce a lack of minority representation and retention. But even institutions committed to improving faculty diversity within their administrative ranks face similar problems. The idea that rich institutional traditions and culture stand in the way of improving faculty diversity is an uncomfortable hypothesis— one deserving of careful consideration all the more so as a result.

There is ample evidence to indicate that conventional efforts to diversify faculty composition and to promote minorities equitably in higher education have failed. Until now, institutions have been largely excused for failing to meet these goals because of their perceived intentions and propensity to mimic the positive practices of peer institutions. Good intentions in addressing the challenge of faculty diversity, however, must be linked to practices that effectively account for institutional culture and norms. Merely relying on the improvement of external circumstances as a possible solution will only lead to another 30 years of woeful underrepresentation of minorities among American faculty and senior administrators.

References

American Association of University Professors (AAUP). (1940). *1940 Statement of principles on academic freedom and tenure.* Retrieved from http://www.aaup.org/AAUP/pubsres/policydocs/contents/1940statement.htm

Bain, O., & Cummings, W. (2000). Academe's glass ceiling: Societal, professional/organizational, and institutional barriers to the career advancement of academic women. *Comparative Education Review, 44*(4), 493–514.

Baldwin, R. G., Lunceford, C. J., & Vanderlinden, K. E. (2005). Faculty in the middle years: Illuminating an overlooked phase of academic life. *The Review of Higher Education, 29*(1), 97–118.

Birnbaum, R. (1988). *How colleges work: The cybernetics of academic organization and leadership.* San Francisco, CA: Jossey-Bass.

Burgan, M. (1998). Academic citizenship: A fading vision. *Liberal Education, 84*(4), 16–21.

Chait, R. P. (Ed.). (2002). *The questions of tenure.* Cambridge, MA: Harvard University Press.

Chernesky, R. H. (2003). Examining the glass ceiling: Gender influences on promotion decisions. *Administration in Social Work, 27*(2), 13–18.

Collie, S. L., & Chronister, J. L. (2001). In search of the next generation of faculty leaders. *Peer Review, 3*(3), 22–23.

Cooper, J. E., & Stevens, D. D. (Eds.). (2002). *Tenure and the sacred grove: Issues and strategies for women and minority faculty.* Albany, NY: SUNY Press.

Eckel, P. D. (Ed.). (2006). *The shifting frontiers of academic decision making: Responding to new priorities, following new pathways.* Lanham, MD: Rowman & Littlefield.

Gappa, J. M., Austin, A. E., & Trice, A. G. (2007). *Rethinking faculty work: Higher education's strategic imperative.* San Francisco, CA: Jossey-Bass.

Gumport, P. J. (2001). Divided we govern? *Peer Review, 3*(3), 14–17.

Ikenberry, S. O. (1971). Restructuring college and university organization and governance: An introduction. *The Journal of Higher Education, 42*(6), 421–429.

Iverson, S. V. (2007). Camouflaging power and privilege: A critical race analysis of university diversity policies. *Educational Administration Quarterly, 43*(5), 586–611.

Jackson, J. F. L. (2008). Race segregation across the academic workforce: Exploring factors that may contribute to the disparate representation of African American men. *American Behavioral Scientist, 51*(7), 1004–1029.

Johnsrud, L. K. (1991). Administrative promotion: The power of gender. *The Journal of Higher Education, 62*(2), 119–149.

Johnsrud, L. K., & Heck, R. H. (1994). Administrative promotion within a university: The cumulative impact of gender. *The Journal of Higher Education, 65*(1), 23–44.

Knapp, L. G., Kelly-Reid, J. E., & Ginder, S. A. (2008). *Employees in postsecondary institutions, fall 2007, and salaries of full-time instructional faculty, 2007–08.* Washington, DC: National Center for Education Statistics, Institute of Education Sciences, U.S. Department of Education.

Kouzes, J. M., & Posner, B. Z. (2003). *The Jossey-Bass academic administrator's guide to exemplary leadership.* San Francisco, CA: Jossey-Bass.

Lee, S. M. (2002). Do Asian American faculty face a glass ceiling? *American Educational Research Journal, 39*(3), 695–724.

McCurtis, B. R., Jackson, J. F. L., & O'Callaghan, E. M. (2009). Developing leaders of color in higher education: Can contemporary programs address historical employment trends? In A. Kezar (Ed.), *New horizons for leadership development for faculty and administrators in higher education* (pp. 65–92). Sterling, VA: Stylus Publishing.

Minor, J. T. (2004). Understanding faculty senates: Moving from mystery to models. *The Review of Higher Education, 27*(3), 343–363.

Mortimer, K. P. (1971). The dilemmas in new campus governance structures. *The Journal of Higher Education, 42*(6), 467–482.

O'Meara, K. (2004). Beliefs about post-tenure review: The influence of autonomy, collegiality, career stage, and institutional context. *The Journal of Higher Education, 75*(2), 178–202.

Orton, J. D., & Weick, K. E. (1990). Loosely coupled systems: A reconceptualization. *The Academy of Management Review, 15*(2), 203–223.

Perna, L. W. (2001). Sex and race differences in faculty tenure and promotion. *Research in Higher Education, 42*(5), 541–567.

Pfnister, A. O. (1970). The role of faculty in university governance. *The Journal of Higher Education, 41*(6), 430–449.

Ryu, M. (2008). *Minorities in higher education 2008: 23rd status report.* Washington, DC: American Council on Education.

Smith, D. G., Turner, C. S., Osei-Kofi, N., & Richards, S. (2004). Interrupting the usual: Successful strategies for hiring minority faculty. *The Journal of Higher Education, 75*(2), 133–160.

Snyder, T. D., Dillow, S. A., & Hoffman, C. M. (2009). *Digest of education statistics 2008.* Washington, DC: National Center for Education Statistics, Institute of Education Sciences, U.S. Department of Education.

Tierney, W. G. (2004). Academic freedom and tenure: Between fiction and reality. *The Journal of Higher Education, 75*(2), 161–177.

Tierney, W. G., & Bensimon, E. M. (1996). *Promotion and tenure: Community and socialization in academe.* Albany, NY: SUNY Press.

Tierney, W. G., & Minor, J. T. (2003). *Challenges for governance: A national report.* Los Angeles, CA: The Center for Higher Education Policy Analysis, Rossier School of Education, The University of Southern California.

Tierney, W. G., & Sallee, M. W. (2008). Do organizational structures and strategies increase faculty diversity?: A cultural analysis. *American Academic, 4*(1), 159–184.

Trower, C. A., & Chait, R. P. (2002). Faculty diversity: Too little for too long. *Harvard Magazine, 104*(2), 33–38.

Turner, C. S. V., & Myers, S. L., Jr. (1999). *Faculty of color in academe: Bittersweet success.* Upper Saddle River, NJ: Pearson.

Weick, K. E. (1976). Educational organizations as loosely coupled systems. *Administrative Science Quarterly, 21*(1), 1–19.

JAMES T. MINOR is the deputy assistant secretary at the U.S. Department of Education.

5

This chapter describes how software technology may be used as an interdisciplinary approach to managing diversity in higher education to mitigate glass ceiling effects.

Using Human Resource Software Technology to Mitigate Glass Ceiling Effects in Higher Education: Interdisciplinary Applications for Managing Diversity

LaVar Jovan Charleston

One of the most significant challenges to workplace diversity in business and higher education is to eradicate barriers to access and advancement for middle- and senior-level employees among underrepresented populations, namely women and minorities. While more than 20 years of research illuminates the prevalence of glass ceiling effects in business and university settings, U.S. trend statistics indicate that women and minorities are achieving representation in upper-level management and senior-level positions in business at rates that exceed those in academia. One explanation for this disparity in representation could be the private sector's innovative use of software technology. This technology is intended to assist Human Resource (HR) managers in measuring diversity and avoiding discriminatory practices, precipitated by the pressure to aggressively address and adhere to affirmative action programs (AAP) and equal employment opportunity (EEO) mandates, as well as the need to avoid litigation.

As the academy is more autonomous and individualized in nature, it is not necessarily under the same type of external pressures as the business sector, yet the need to advance diversity and mitigate glass ceiling effects remains. This chapter is organized around interdisciplinary approaches to managing diversity, identifying key software technology, generally used by HR managers in the private sector, as a potentially useful tool for mitigating glass ceiling effects within higher education.

Amid increased global competition, the United States retains a unique competitive advantage if it learns to leverage workforce diversity properly

NEW DIRECTIONS FOR INSTITUTIONAL RESEARCH, no. 159 © 2014 Wiley Periodicals, Inc.
Published online in Wiley Online Library (wileyonlinelibrary.com) • DOI: 10.1002/ir.20054

(Cox & Smolinski, 1994). While the United States is the most diverse nation among the major industrial countries in the world, a failure to effectively manage racial, ethnic, and other differences serves as a potential threat to its economic viability, particularly given that minorities comprise an increasing share of the population. Historically, discriminatory practices have been a major impediment to successfully achieving diverse workforces in business and higher education alike. But less obvious discriminatory practices in particular—referred to as "glass ceiling effects" for the purposes of this chapter—provide White males with disproportionate advantages in terms of: (a) pay, (b) salary increases, (c) hiring, (d) training and development, and (e) promotions (Lockwood, 2004).

While studies have identified glass ceiling effects in a variety of disciplines within the United States, their prevalence is perhaps most pronounced within academia (Center for Women's Business Research, 2004; Jackson & O'Callaghan, 2009; Morrison & Von Glinow, 1990). Although the federal government acknowledged the glass ceiling as a barrier to the advancement of women and people of color in the workplace more than 20 years ago (Federal Glass Ceiling Commission, 1995a, 1995b; Jackson & O'Callaghan, 2009; Martin, 1991, 1992), the lack of a consistent, discipline-wide definition of glass ceiling practices and their effects has contributed to a lack of empirical research on glass ceiling effects within academia (Jackson & O'Callaghan, 2009).

As businesses and organizations continue to undergo dramatic changes in form and function, researchers increasingly look to concepts such as innovation, emergence, and improvisation to explain how technology is employed in practice (Orlikowski, 2000). Some findings indicate that the incorporation and use of technology in higher education is associated with increased educational gains and outcomes, but this body of literature generally emphasizes student learning or faculty instruction (Flowers, 2004; Kuh & Hu, 2001; Strayhorn, 2007) with little to no attention paid to higher education administrators' use of technology to diversify university campuses or departments.

In contrast, the development and use of technology by business and HR managers in the private sector has been a subject of some scholarly attention. The federal government's push to numerically rate HR performance, research and study diversity, evaluate compliance with AAP, and enforce EEO is believed to have facilitated the adoption and development of new technologies among business and HR managers (Stutz & Massengale, 1997). Differences in external pressures could explain differences in technology use among managers and administrators between the two sectors. Likewise, this variation could also explain the apparent differential in progress toward mitigating glass ceiling effects across business and academia.

In order to advance the study of glass ceiling effects in higher education, more work is required to qualify and quantify these effects (Jackson

& O'Callaghan, 2009). While some empirical research specifically identifies and investigates diversity management with regard to glass ceiling effects in higher education (e.g., Cotter, Hermsen, Ovadia, & Vanneman, 2001; Jackson & O'Callaghan, 2009; Maume, 2004), there is a growing need for measures that quantify the prevalence of such effects within the academic workforce—in order to mitigate their consequences. With underrepresented groups gaining increased representation in senior-level management and leadership positions in business (Jackson & O'Callaghan, 2009), examining HR management within the business sector may illuminate innovative solutions and practices that higher education administrators might find useful.

To date, Jackson and O'Callaghan (2009) offer the most comprehensive review of glass ceiling effects in higher education. The researchers argue that the term "glass ceiling," popular in conversational vernacular, lacks a clear definition for use in research. In addition to the absence of scholarship exploring the intersection of race, ethnicity, gender, and glass ceiling effects, there is also a dearth of research focused on national employment trends for the academic workforce and, more specifically, senior-level administration within it. Additional research on glass ceiling effects in higher education is needed to investigate, identify, and quantify these effects in a manner that would be broadly generalizable to academic departments around the country and even the world.

The research questions that guide this chapter are: (a) How is diversity managed outside of higher education?; (b) How is diversity measured outside of higher education?; (c) How can higher education quantify glass ceiling effects?; (d) How can innovative technologies be used to mitigate glass ceiling effects?; and (e) What can academia learn from other disciplines with regard to the measurement and mitigation of glass ceiling effects?

Method

To situate this chapter within the body of existing literature, a review of relevant research was conducted concerning glass ceilings, technology, diversity, and higher education. Manuscripts from the years 1988–2009 were gathered from electronic databases and yielded results from a variety of disciplinary fields and scholarly publications.

Due to the interdisciplinary nature of this study, the database search yielded few results that spoke to the uses of software technology to manage diversity and glass ceiling effects within higher education. Instead, the selected publications that were examined for this inquiry illuminated specific disciplinary concepts applicable to this chapter's research questions. Additionally, the author utilizes Dass and Parker's (1999) General Framework for Managing Diversity as a conceptual model. Although this framework is generally applied to private sector executive management, here it is used with respect to managing diversity among the occupational levels of academia.

Figure 5.1. General Framework for Managing Diversity

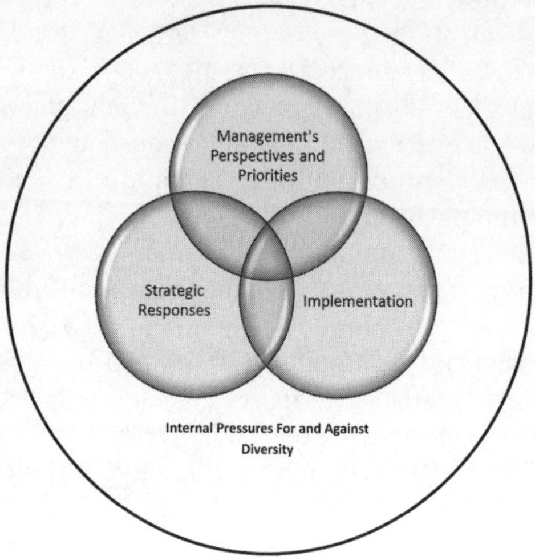

Source: Adapted from Dass and Parker's (1999) General Framework for Managing Diversity.

Conceptual Framework

Dass and Parker's (1999) General Framework for Managing Diversity highlights the link between executives, organizational conditions, and performance managing workforce diversity. It asserts that, for all practical purposes, most organizations within the United States amass more diverse workforces as a response to external and/or internal pressures (see Figure 5.1). For example,

> Customers, suppliers, civil liberties groups, or those representing social, legal, economic, and other imperatives might exert external pressures to hire more people of color. At the same time, diversity champions, employee groups, or change managers might apply internal pressures for diversity in organizational hiring. (Dass & Parker, 1999, p. 68)

The researchers emphasize how managers' perspectives, priorities, and strategic responses—as they relate to diversity initiatives, objectives, and/or the lack thereof—are attributable to pressures specific to the managers' governing organizations. In other words, the decisions they make affect strategic responses, implementation, and, potentially, diversity-related pressures (Dass & Parker, 1999). In fact, the variety of legal and ethical lenses through which diversity is viewed fosters variation in its definition, how it is studied, and how it is approached in workplace settings (Cox & Smolinski, 1994; Dass & Parker, 1999). Likewise, these variations foster glass ceiling effects that are more prevalent in some sectors of the U.S. economy, such as higher education, than in others, such as business, particularly as it relates to senior-level staffing (Center for Women's Business Research, 2004).

Dass and Parker (1999) incorporate examples from U.S., European, and Japanese firms to inform their General Framework for Managing Diversity, specifically examining businesses where social, legal, cultural, and competitive pressures combined to necessitate increased diversity in: (a) personnel, (b) organizational structures, and (c) processes. As institutions of higher education are expected to produce the next generation of leaders in an increasingly diverse and global economy, all ranks within academia should be as diverse as the populations they serve. As such, the academy ought to conform to the notion that "ideal transnational firms will be those whose strategic capabilities include global competitiveness, flexibility, and worldwide learning, capabilities that are enhanced by high degrees of human diversity in organization" (Dass & Parker, 1999, p. 78). In an effort to achieve this goal, executives and higher education administrators must reflect on their own diversity practices. Doing so will foster an increased awareness of assumptions and biases that may further guide individual practices and theories—particularly in regard to hiring and promotion (Dass & Parker, 1999)—as well as mitigate glass ceiling effects in higher education.

Diversity and the Glass Ceiling Within Academia

Although 30 years of affirmative action and EEO policies have resulted in more diverse colleges and universities, the vast majority of American faculty remain largely White and male (Trower & Chait, 2002). Males comprise 84% of presidents, 83% of business officers, and 75% of academic deans in higher education (Corrigan, 2002; Jackson & O'Callaghan, 2009). Men and women of color have consistently held lower academic ranks than Whites, accounting for only 11% of full professors (Trower & Chait, 2002). Additionally, among CEOs on college campuses, just 9% are African American, 2% are American Indian, 0.1% are Asian American, and 5% are Hispanic, while 84% are White. This statistic highlights a significant underrepresentation of leadership positions among minorities and people of color as compared to national population-trend statistics (Jackson & O'Callaghan, 2009).

While representation of faculty of color increased from the years 1989–1997, women of color who attained full professor status constitute 23.2% of all women faculty members and men of color who attained the same status constitute just 9% of all male faculty members. Only 2.5% of these women of color and 8% of these men of color, however, held full professorships, as compared with 17% of White women and 72% of White men (Trower & Chait, 2002). These stark statistics have precipitated the study of the glass ceiling within higher education, with the majority of these studies (Glazer-Raymo, 1999; Jackson & O'Callaghan, 2009) showing a disproportionate lack of representation in senior-level positions as demonstrated through demographic and employment data for women and minorities at colleges and universities.

Exploring Interdisciplinary Alternatives

The relatively miniscule gains for women and minorities within senior leadership positions in academia suggest alternative approaches to mitigating these glass ceiling effects are needed. In the business world, HR professionals are frequently placed in leadership positions that enable them to have a broad impact on their organization (Lockwood, 2004). According to Lockwood (2004), it is imperative for such HR managers to be knowledgeable about the glass ceiling phenomenon for it might directly or indirectly impact an organization's reputation, customer loyalty, diversity of skill sets, growth potential, and bottom line. As they are required to be knowledgeable about employment laws, programs, and practices for their organizations, they maintain responsibilities to understand the potential impact of glass ceiling barriers.

Additionally, other factors, such as the Office of Federal Contract Compliance Program's (OFCCP) numerical goals for written AAP, have increased the need for employers to track statistical data on their workforce demographics (Stutz & Massengale, 1997). Consequently, specialists in EEO and affirmative action are routinely exploring innovative ways to measure the performance of HR departments' efforts to communicate organizational change in a clear and concise manner. In turn, the need to generate and analyze diversity data has been a catalyst for the development of diversity measurement software used by HR practitioners at national, top-level business organizations, like Microsoft (Stutz & Massengale, 1997).

Diversity Measurement Software

There is a range of diversity measurement software available referred to by the Equal Employment Opportunity Commission (EEOC). Most of these software applications facilitate the use of statistical analysis in reporting results. These software technologies are used for a variety of purposes and can be categorized in two ways: preemptive software (software to inform organizations where they stand in regard to their diversity goals) and reactive software (software to inform litigation of discriminatory practices). The following section will showcase an example of such diversity measurement software, how it is used, and how it can be adapted by academic administrators to assist in the mitigation of glass ceiling effects.

EEOSTAT. EEOSTAT is a software tool created by a practicing attorney with over 30 years of litigating experience concerning discrimination at the federal and appellate levels (Bannon, n.d.-a). The software, assisting in the quantification of employment law, assesses whether or not employment decisions present patterns that could be evidence of discriminatory practices within a company or an organization. EEOSTAT is comprised of three components that enable the statistical evaluation of diversity-related employment processes: (a) EEOSTAT: Square, (b) EEOSTAT: Avail, and (c) EEOSTAT: Paycalc. As academia does not typically follow a unified pay scale, in-depth explanation of EEOSTAT: Paycalc (Bannon, n.d.-c) will be omitted in this chapter.

   EEOSTAT: Square. Square is a quantitative test of selections from a pool of applicants that calculates the statistical significance of disparities in employment-selection processes when applicant flow data are available. The tool computes probability values using a Chi-square test and, for 2 × 2 tables, Fisher's Exact Test. For example, in a race/hiring case, Square determines if there is a significant disparity in the rates at which Blacks and Whites are hired. When this probability is sufficiently low (e.g., 0.05 or less), the result is typically considered statistically significant and thus generally recognized as evidence of discrimination (Bannon, n.d.-d).

   The following is an example of how EEOSTAT: Square works (see Figure 5.2). A charge has been filed against the XYZ Co. alleging racial discrimination in hiring processes. About 16% of Black applicants were hired as compared with 38% of White applicants. Square shows this disparity to be statistically significant, with a probability of 3 in 10,000 for the two-tail Fisher's Exact Test. As a rule, probabilities less than 0.05, or 5 in 100, are considered statistically significant.

   EEOSTAT: Avail. Avail is a quantitative test of selection that does not rely on the availability of hiring data. It calculates the statistical significance of disparities in an employment-selection process when there is no applicant flow data and when protected class availability has been estimated from Census or other labor market data. The tool calculates probabilities using the exact binomial and the normal approximation to the binomial tests, and similar to Square, any computed, statistically significant disparities are typically recognized as evidence of discrimination (Bannon, n.d.-b).

   The following is an example of how the EEOSTAT: Avail software works (see Figure 5.3). The ABC Co. hired 245 drivers, 21 of whom were women. It has been estimated that 17% of the local labor market for drivers is female. Avail calculates that there is a shortfall of about 21 female hires (21.38) and accordingly that this disparity is statistically significant. For the two-tail exact binomial test, the probability is 0.0001, or about 1 chance in 10,000. As before, probabilities less than 0.05, or 5 in 100 are generally considered statistically significant.

   These examples illustrate how diversity measurement software can be used to shed light on what might be considered discriminatory business practices. Within the context of academia, similarly designed software could be used to illuminate what might be deemed glass ceiling effects. However, as Dass and Parker's (1999) General Framework for Managing Diversity suggests, adequate internal and external pressures are necessary to compel

NEW DIRECTIONS FOR INSTITUTIONAL RESEARCH • DOI: 10.1002/ir

Figure 5.2.   EEOSTAT: Square

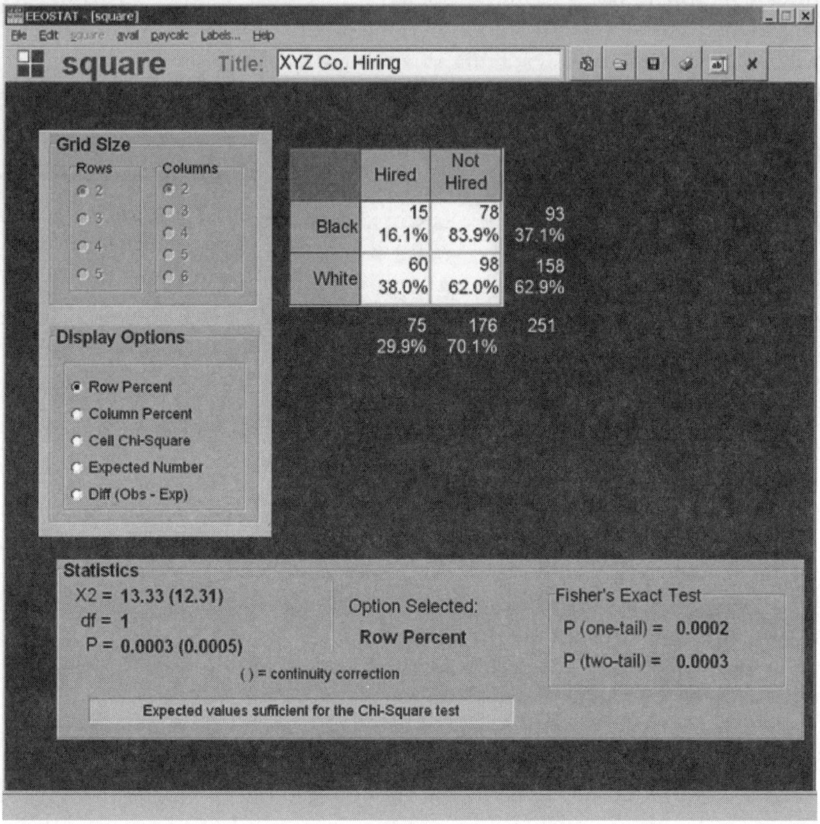

Source: Reprinted from https://www.eeostat.com/eeostat/square/

administrators to make use of these additional tools aimed at addressing glass ceiling effects.

Many educational institutions of higher learning boast of a commitment to diversity, which might contribute to some external and internal pressures to better demonstrate their performance. Within the General Framework for Managing Diversity (Dass & Parker, 1999), the implementation of software technology to aid in diversity initiatives could serve to provide quantitative measures by which glass ceiling effects are identified, addressed, and corrected. While the autonomous nature of academia tends to mean practices are often subject to less accountability, diversity measurement software helps promote transparency. It enables the assessment of hiring and promotion practices fostering greater accountability with respect to the fulfillment of diversity goals and objectives.

NEW DIRECTIONS FOR INSTITUTIONAL RESEARCH • DOI: 10.1002/ir

Figure 5.3. EEOSTAT: Avail

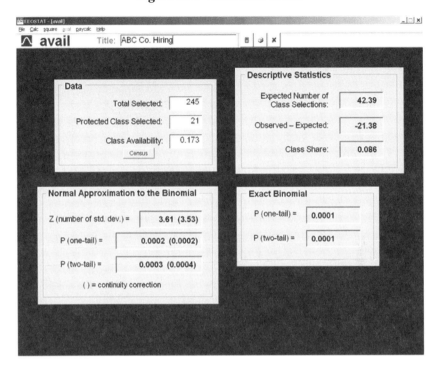

Source: Reprinted from https://www.eeostat.com/eeostat/avail/

Conclusions and Implications

While many businesses, organizations, and higher education institutions emphasize diversity and its benefits, women and minorities still overwhelmingly feel the effects of the glass ceiling; they remain underrepresented in upper-level positions in academia. But diversity measurement software, generally designed for HR practitioners in the business sector, can be tailored specifically for use in higher education administration, in order to better mitigate glass ceiling effects within academia.

Still, pressures that encourage diversity measurement in business are not equally shared by academia. The federal government's efforts to quantify HR performance and track diversity and compliance with the EEOC directly contributes to the development and use of innovative software by business and HR managers (Stutz & Massengale, 1997). The private sector's more aggressive stance with regard to diversity explains their superior progress relative to academia. Administrators in higher education seeking to mirror this positive trend, as evidenced by national employment data, need to look no further than the improved standing of underrepresented groups in senior-level management and business leadership positions (Jackson &

O'Callaghan, 2009) and the innovative solutions and practices employed to achieve those results. Specifically, academic administrators ought to emulate the private sector's use of software technology providing quantitative measures of diversity that can aid in advancing hiring initiatives to counter the effects of glass ceiling practices.

Though this chapter presented examples using EEOSTAT software, it does not necessarily advocate the use of this particular diversity measurement software. Instead, these examples are meant to identify diversity measurement software as a legitimate tool that not only provides a means to assess diversity and glass ceiling effects, but one that also affords administrators a mechanism for evaluating institutional and departmental performance toward achieving diversity-related objectives. Therefore, this chapter underlines the importance of partnerships between software designers, higher education administrators, and proponents of diversity. Because managing diversity entails conscientious efforts to counteract glass ceiling effects, administrators must aggressively pursue diversity by bringing underrepresented individuals into higher education and by promoting them at levels that match their White counterparts.

The wealth of resources available to academia provides administrators with immediate access to software designers for the sake of developing department-specific, diversity measurement software that suits individualized sectors of the academic community. Thus, while this chapter presents a technological solution to a social problem, administrators must still assume a great deal of accountability. Ultimately, the use of these technologies must translate to aggressive action in the name of mitigating these glass ceiling effects.

References

Bannon, J. C. (n.d.-a). *EEOSTAT: Statistical software for employment law*. Retrieved from http://www.eeostat.com
Bannon, J. C. (n.d.-b). *EEOSTAT: Avail*. Retrieved from http://www.eeostat.com /avail
Bannon, J. C. (n.d.-c). *EEOSTAT: Paycalc*. Retrieved from http://www.eeostat.com /paycalc
Bannon, J. C. (n.d.-d). *EEOSTAT: Square*. Retrieved from http://www.eeostat.com/square
Center for Women's Business Research. (2004). *Businesses owned by women of color in the United States*. Washington, DC: Author.
Corrigan, M. E. (2002). *The American college president*. Washington, DC: The American Council on Education Center for Policy Analysis.
Cotter, D. A., Hermsen, J. M., Ovadia, S., & Vanneman, R. (2001). The glass ceiling effect. *Social Forces, 80*(2), 655–681.
Cox, T., Jr., & Smolinski, C. (1994). *Managing diversity and glass ceiling initiatives as national economic imperatives*. Washington, DC: U.S. Department of Labor.
Dass, P., & Parker, B. (1999). Strategies for managing human resource diversity: From resistance to learning. *The Academy of Management Executive, 13*(2), 68–80.
Federal Glass Ceiling Commission. (1995a). *Good for business: Making full use of the nation's human capital*. Washington, DC: U.S. Department of Labor.

Federal Glass Ceiling Commission. (1995b). *A solid investment: Making full use of the nation's human capital.* Washington, DC: U.S. Department of Labor.

Flowers, L. A. (2004). Analyzing the impact of email use on student-faculty interactions in higher education programs. *Student Affairs Online, 5*(4). Retrieved from http://studentaffairs.com/ejournal/Fall_2004/ImpactofEmail.html

Glazer-Raymo, J. (1999). *Shattering the myths: Women in academe.* Baltimore, MD: Johns Hopkins University Press.

Jackson, J. F. L., & O'Callaghan, E. M. (2009). What do we know about glass ceiling effects? A taxonomy and critical review to inform higher education research. *Research in Higher Education, 50*(5), 460–482.

Kuh, G. D., & Hu, S. (2001). The relationship between computer and information technology use, selected learning and personal development outcomes, and other college experiences. *Journal of College Student Development, 42*(3), 217–232.

Lockwood, N. R. (2004). *The glass ceiling: Domestic and international perspectives.* Alexandria, VA: Society for Human Resource Management.

Martin, L. (1991). *A report on the glass ceiling commission.* Washington, DC: U.S. Department of Labor.

Martin, L. (1992). *Pipelines of progress—A status report on the glass ceiling.* Washington, DC: U.S. Department of Labor.

Maume, D. J., Jr. (2004). Is the glass ceiling a unique form of inequality? Evidence from a random-effects model of managerial attainment. *Work and Occupations, 31*(2), 250–274.

Morrison, A. M., & Von Glinow, M. A. (1990). Women and minorities in management. *American Psychologist, 45*(2), 200–208.

Orlikowski, W. J. (2000). Using technology and constituting structures: A practice lens for studying technology in organizations. *Organization Science, 11*(4), 404–428.

Strayhorn, T. L. (2007). Use of technology among higher education faculty members: Implications for innovative practice. *Student Affairs Online, 8*(2). Retrieved from http://studentaffairs.com/ejournal/Summer_2007/TechnologyUseByFaculty.html

Stutz, J., & Massengale, R. (1997). Measuring diversity initiatives. *HRMagazine, 42*, 85–90.

Trower, C. A., & Chait, R. P. (2002). Faculty diversity: Too little for too long. *Harvard Magazine, 104*, 23–28.

LAVAR JOVAN CHARLESTON is the assistant director and a senior research associate at Wisconsin's Equity and Inclusion Laboratory (Wei LAB) at the University of Wisconsin-Madison.

6

This chapter centers on the challenges of translating glass ceiling research findings into meaningful organizational change initiatives, moving from theory or scholarship to practice.

Organizational Learning as a Framework for Overcoming Glass Ceiling Effects in Higher Education

Damon A. Williams

While more women and people of color occupy leadership positions in higher education than ever before, the top of the career ladder remains inaccessible for diverse groups. The glass ceiling—that barrier preventing specific populations from advancing to administrative levels—has been part of the management lexicon for some time. This lack of racial and gender diversity at the senior levels of institutions is partially a result of glass ceiling effects that have resulted in a higher education landscape where only 23% of college presidents are women and 14% ethnic and racially diverse minorities (Nealy, 2008).

Other chapters in this volume focus on best practices of research techniques for studying, analyzing, and understanding glass ceiling effects. This chapter, on the other hand, centers on the monumental challenges of translating research findings into meaningful organizational change initiatives, moving from theory or scholarship to practice. Part of the difficulty in bridging this divide lies in the increasing evolution of higher education as a pure research discipline that has become disconnected from the administrative world of practice. As Kezar (2000) eloquently describes, higher education research has changed from a domain of educational administrators to a more discipline-based, theory-laden field, one less relevant to practitioners. This mismatch undoubtedly plays a role in the failure to apply what researchers have learned about glass ceiling effects, yet it does not completely explain them.

This chapter focuses on the processes of overcoming glass ceiling effects, which require researchers and others to understand institutional barriers to change and actively work to overcome them. It is grounded in the experiences of the author, who has been a leader in a higher education chief

NEW DIRECTIONS FOR INSTITUTIONAL RESEARCH, no. 159 © 2014 Wiley Periodicals, Inc.
Published online in Wiley Online Library (wileyonlinelibrary.com) • DOI: 10.1002/ir.20055

diversity officer division, as well as relevant literature in this area and findings from a mixed method research project entitled "The Chief Diversity Officer Study," which was conducted by the author (Williams & Wade-Golden, 2008).

Understanding Institutional Culture

Research into glass ceiling effects illustrates trends such as failures to cast broad enough nets in external searches, tendencies to hire exclusively from homogenous internal pools, salary compression, and/or pernicious cycles of negatively evaluating women and minority candidates under the aegis of not being good institutional "fits." Yet when these data are presented, what happens next? Are they translated into strategies for meaningful change that will diversify senior ranks of an institution? How does this information lead to tactics that will aggressively advance an institution's diversity agenda?

Too often, institutional research professionals, diversity planning committees, faculty, staff, and diversity officers will author comprehensive diversity reports that illuminate such challenges—in this case, the dynamics of glass ceiling effects—but ultimately fail to propose clear strategies of action, change management, and accountability. To take meaningful steps to overcome glass ceiling effects, institutional research professionals and others must become strategic diversity leaders, versed in the ideas of organizational learning and change (Argyris & Schon, 1974; Paul, 2003; Senge, 1990; Williams, 2013). Any philosophy of diversity leadership must learn from past mistakes, build on prior successes, ask hard questions, and move beyond flawed approaches that yield suboptimal results.

After 30 years of affirmative action programs and diversity training efforts, any success with regard to mitigating glass ceiling effects will hinge less on an understanding of issues of diversity and more on understanding the processes of organizational change. This fact is necessary whether one is an institutional researcher, department chair, or chief diversity officer. More colleges and universities must operate as learning institutions concerned with building real solutions to alter the state of these dynamics (Smith, Turner, Osei-Kofi, & Richards, 2004).

Schein (2004) theorizes that organizational cultures contain multiple overlapping layers. The culture is easy to see, manipulate, and change at the outermost level, the "geospatial level." Processes of change associated with this level are generally undertaken through first-order simple strategies and might include relocating a multicultural center to the heart of campus or developing a new mural in a student union "heritage room" that depicts multicultural life. By comparison, more resilient aspects of culture exist at deeper levels, embedded in mental models and individual perceptions of diversity, excellence, and inclusion (Williams, Berger, & McClendon, 2005). For some, these deeper levels equate administrative diversification to a "lessening of quality" and "establishing quotas." Consequently, many institutional symbols, myths, traditions, processes, and behaviors do not affirm diversity but rather create a "culture of resistance" that presents a monumental challenge to diversity efforts (Alger, 2009).

Shifting Institutional Culture

Researchers have since begun to approach the idea of resistance in less linear terms, focusing on how positive intentions can lead to negative reactions to change (Piderit, 2000). Furthermore, these negative reactions may not be present at the outset but emerge unexpectedly as the process unfolds (Feldman, 2004), occurring not in the context of a single organizational culture but rather a set of diverse and sometimes competing subcultures (Jermier, Slocum, Fry, & Gaines, 1991). Understanding this multidimensional resistance is an important first step in determining how best to implement diversity innovations.

Many of the actions of traditional institutional planning efforts take place at the incremental level, seldom reshaping patterns of thinking and behaving. Such actions rarely occur at a transformational level, shifting the context or point of view around a single issue. These factors of resistance are not unique to academia, but, when manifested together in a milieu heavily steeped in tradition, academic freedom, and autonomy, they produce a synergistic effect of working against meaningful change. What follows in the next section is a description of several dynamics upon which institutional researchers and others must focus to overcome glass ceiling effects: (a) the challenge of fit, (b) the lack of diversity accountability systems, and (c) ingrained hiring practices.

The Challenge of Fit.   One of the most powerful factors opposing organizational change is a cluster of preconceptions that constitute a potential faculty or staff member's fit with an institution. In some instances, search and screen committees make concerted efforts to ensure that job announcements reach diverse audiences and result in diverse applicant pools, only for these proactive efforts to be derailed by preconceived notions: which institutions produce the best graduates, what activities best predict candidates' potential, and, perhaps most damaging, evaluation of a candidates' favorable or unfavorable personal characteristics, all under the egis of institutional fit.

More often than not, these criteria are based on principles that fail to embrace diversity as adding value to an institution. A growing body of research highlights the organizational performance and learning benefits of a diverse environment (Cox, 2001; Milem, Chang, & Antonio, 2005); however, in this instance, difference is viewed as detrimental unless it is wrapped within a preferred demographic and personality profile. For example, women and people of color are sometimes excluded based upon cultural styles of communication, often labeled as overly emotional, loud, or aggressive (Parker, 2001). These tendencies, long discussed in diversity management literature (Cox, 2001; Parker, 2001), often lead to such individuals being stereotyped as difficult to work with, unprofessional, incompetent, or even scary. One chief diversity officer interviewed as part of the Chief Diversity Officer Study explained:

> The president, a White male scientist, was hired for his role even though ethnic and racial minorities and women were staunchly against his candidacy, finding his communication style to be dismissive and at times demeaning to diverse groups. But as chief diversity officer, and more importantly, as an African-American woman, I was told that my colleagues did not like me, and that I needed to build better relationships with them, if I was going to be successful in my role. (Williams & Wade-Golden, 2007)

Implicit in this comment is that it is acceptable for a White male to be unpopular but not a person of color.

Furthermore, Dovidio, Glick, and Rudman (2005) argue that this type of subtle bias is grounded in processes of social categorization and cultural stereotyping that justify persistent racism and minority exclusion. They contend that individuals naturally devalue groups different from their own, often and spontaneously, usually based upon race and gender without conscious motivation. This concept is referred to as "aversive racism," a subtle form of bias endemic to many White Americans that is largely context-specific, for aversive racists do not discriminate against minorities in situations where discrimination would be obvious to others and themselves.

Aversive racists, however, do discriminate, usually unintentionally and in subtle ways that can be easily rationalized: (a) when a negative response can be justified on the basis of a factor other than race, (b) when evaluative criteria are ambiguous, or (c) when providing special favors or support to ingroup members rather than denograting or criticizing outgroup members (Dovidio et al., 2005).

As such, aversive racists display subtle discrimination in response to direct or symbolic threats to the status quo, showing less acceptance of or support for high-status versus low-status minorities (Dovidio et al., 2005). These subtle dynamics of exclusion often power the conversation of fit when search and screen committees make stereotypical assumptions about candidates' preferences, social needs, or professional or personal aspirations. A committee will assume, for instance, that a person of color will not be happy in a small, predominantly White college town, or that a woman of a certain age is planning to start a family, thus limiting the amount of time she will be able to work (Alger, 2009). This discrimination is particularly problematic because it assumes the best interests of candidates and discourages committees from examining their own prejudices.

Unfortunately, approaches for combating traditional forms of racism are generally ineffective in contending with aversive racism. Providing colorblind equal opportunity, in particular, may be unsuccessful. Aversive racists are not colorblind; on the contrary, a growing body of research demonstrates that Whites immediately categorize minorities on the basis of race, automatically self-activating negative stereotypes and attitudes (Dovidio et al., 2005). As a consequence, bias continues at the personal level or in policies that subtly disadvantage minorities by failing to provide them with the same support or benefit of the doubt that White men often receive. Accordingly, these notions must be addressed by institutional research professionals, diversity leaders, and, most importantly, leadership at committee, department, and senior leadership levels, not only when discussing fit but also when implementing glass ceiling effects research.

Lack of Diversity Accountability. Institutional accountability is yet another factor that contributes to a lack of diversity. National data taken from the aforementioned study on chief diversity officers (Williams & Wade-Golden, 2008) show that only 21% of institutions considered diversity-related leadership activities as part of the merit reviews of administrators, and only 10% when reviewing faculty. These findings illustrate the ways in which institutions have failed to integrate powerful diversity accountability systems into strategies of change.

As a result, top leadership tend to rely heavily on persuasion to initiate new diversity innovations, often perceiving the enforcement of these directives as overly punitive. Ironically, when accountability is infused into diversity implementation activities, it usually takes the form of reporting on campus diversity efforts. For example, 51% of institutions in the chief diversity officer database indicate that they regularly report on their institution's diversity challenges and successes (Williams & Wade-Golden, 2008). Yet chief diversity officers were much less certain of the strategies they were employing when asked about the consequences of less-than-successful diversity implementations. Hence, the majority of institutions have diversity policies that, while well-intentioned, bear little or no teeth.

The reluctance to engage in activities that promote diversity points to deeper, underlying attitudes about the lack of perceived value of diversity in general. Faculty and deans are subject to any number of accountability exercises such as grant reporting, reaccreditation processes, and departmental self-studies, all of which are usually accepted with little to no resistance. This fact could perhaps be attributed to the connection between these activities and institutional and individual status as well as the financial rewards that flow from receiving grants, publishing scientific findings, and other direct or indirect benefits. The rewards of a diverse university, however, are less apparent and, as such, accountability strategies are often met with more resistance.

Ingrained Hiring Practices. A third and final facet of higher education institutional dynamics relates to hiring practices. Universities go to great lengths to use nondiscriminatory language in job postings and to advertise in publications inclusive of minority audiences, such as *Diverse Issues in Higher Education* and *Hispanic Outlook*. Outreach efforts, however, often stop here. Effective recruitment requires doing far more than posting job descriptions, an ultimately symbolic action of diversification that will not shift the ethnic and gender composition of institutional management teams.

Search committees frequently use the existing landscape of their own institutions as a single litmus test for evaluating candidates rather than considering how to evolve organizational culture. They try to replicate the qualities of the individual they are replacing or, alternatively, rely on established signals of excellence, such as publishing in specific journals or favoring certain teaching and service activities. One of the most familiar and unquestioned criteria is the ranking of a candidate's graduate school; this metric is particularly problematic since students of color often receive PhDs from historically black colleges and universities (HBCUs), which tend to score lower rankings (Alger, 2009). These traditional measurements of merit have value, but they are not the only standards by which to gauge talent, accomplishments, and potential.

To build outstanding leadership teams, academic search committees must heed the lessons of athletics and business. Higher education must aggressively pursue the best and the brightest candidates, wherever they can be found. Administrators must aggressively coach and develop diverse faculty in an effort to help them mature and emerge as department leaders, capable of producing new vectors of potential in their scholarship and assuming new leadership mantles at all levels within their institutions. Leaders must be more aggressive if they wish to diversify administrative ranks and overcome those glass ceiling effects that exist on campuses. Combined, these three factors work together to stanch diversity within the junior ranks of higher education faculty and staff, circumscribing who can compete for and eventually ascend into senior leadership positions.

Organizational Learning as Framework for Resistance to Change

When facing deeply embedded factors that contribute to resistance to change, the challenge of institutional transformation may seem insurmountable. There is, however, a growing body of evidence to suggest that tapping into the theory of organizational learning can shift these dynamics from reactive to proactive, dysfunctional to functional, drawing on a shared sense of purpose rather than a clash of competing values and needs (Paul, 2003; Scharmer, 2007; Senge, 1990). As a framework for better understanding how to situate the needs inherent in any university's diversity agenda, organizational learning allows changes to take root at the origins of the problem, to address underlying and systemic issues rather than excessively concentrating on surface concerns, which are easily seen but also easily papered over within a given culture (Paul, 2003; Scharmer, 2007; Senge, 1990).

NEW DIRECTIONS FOR INSTITUTIONAL RESEARCH • DOI: 10.1002/ir

Figure 6.1. Triple-Loop Model of Organizational Learning

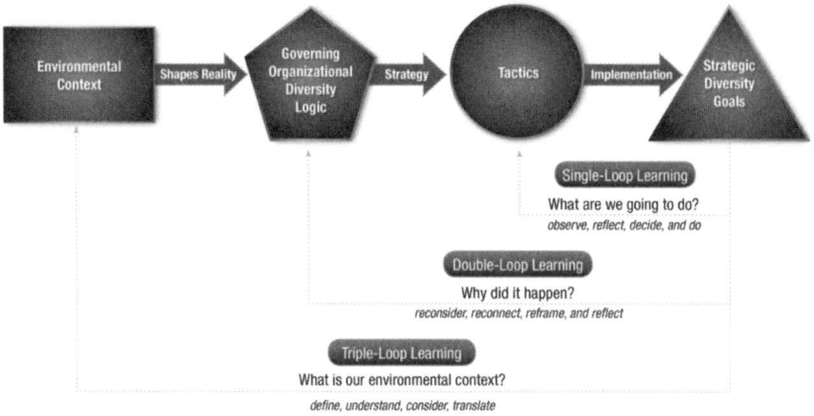

Source: Williams (2013).

Organizational Learning Loops. The concept of the learning organization provides a model for understanding the challenge of translating glass ceiling effects research into practice. Senge's (1990) *The Fifth Discipline* popularized this idea, describing the learning organization as a place where people, both individually and collectively, expand their capacities to create change by continually sharing, processing, and translating information into new actions and outcomes they care about. Accordingly, cause and effect are thought of as something that emerges from a multiplicity of factors, generated from multiple organizational levels and seemingly unrelated causes. Simple solutions bring about limited or short-term success or fail altogether (Senge, 1990; Senge, Kleiner, Roberts, Ross, & Smith, 1994). Organizational learning then, as depicted in Figure 6.1, focuses on how institutions gather and process information in single, double, and triple "organizational learning loops."

Single-Loop Learning. When organizational challenges are detected or less-than-satisfactory diversity outcomes are apparent, actions are initiated that, despite implementation, continue to produce static results. This type of error-and-correction process is "single-loop learning." Single-loop organizational learning strategies focus on minor fixes and adjustments, leaving deeper and more fundamental issues unaddressed: the challenge of fit, the lack of diversity accountability systems, and entrenched hiring methods. Leaders operating in the single loop are primarily concerned with questions such as, "What are we going to do now, given the outcomes that we achieved?" and "How can we achieve new outcomes without shifting existing norms?"

Double-Loop Learning. By comparison, "double-loop learning" occurs when an error is corrected in ways that involve modification of an organization's underlying norms, values, and beliefs that guide how institutions behave. Individuals maintain beliefs as to what constitutes "good" candidates or prefer those candidates who have had similar experiences to their own. For example, one might believe that the only individual who will make a good provost must come through the ranks: junior faculty, tenured faculty, department chair, associate dean, dean, and finally provost. To reach new outcomes, though, it is necessary to address these underlying assumptions and rethink the governing organizational logic that guides strategy and tactics with regard to institutional diversity goals.

Double-loop organizational learning is also a process of reflection in which entities—individuals, groups, or organizations—consider why particular courses of action were chosen over other possibilities. The central question of strategic diversity leaders operating within a double-loop learning mindset then becomes, "Why did this happen, given the outcomes that we achieved?" Finding answers and consequently marshaling the courage to act in a bold new direction is the difference between meaningful diversity efforts that are potentially transformative and those that are woefully disappointing. If institutional search committees are not held accountable for looking creatively at talent with diversity in mind, then how can individuals be expected to arrive at this conclusion on their own without requirements, training, incentives, higher expectations, and real-world consequences? As such, double-loop learning stands as a foundational key to developing sound strategies and tactical actions that will allow institutions to overcome glass ceiling effects.

Triple-Loop Learning.   Triple-loop learning occurs at three levels; it involves not only tactical thinking (single loop) and guiding organizational logic (double loop), but also the big-picture strategic context of a given institution. It involves the active consideration of an institution's surrounding environment and its strategic reality as a new organizational logic to be harnessed in driving strategy and action forward. This chapter proposes, then, that institutional transformation becomes possible when triple-loop organization occurs.

This mode of learning asks, "What is the organizational context? What is the big picture?" The clearest examples of triple-loop strategic diversity thinking occur when dramatic shifts transpire in policy. Here, the focus is on defining the environment, assessing the larger context, and translating it into a new understanding of what should be done to achieve strategic diversity goals. As diversity leaders operate at multiple levels, engaging each of the organizational loops, institutional researchers can shape change by helping administrative and faculty leaders understand the differences between "incremental adjustments" (single-loop strategies), "reframing" (double-loop strategies), and "transformational learning" (triple-loop strategies).

Conclusion

To truly overcome glass ceiling effects in the academy, researchers and administrators must develop a clear understanding of the challenges that impede progress and develop strategies accordingly. As outlined in this chapter, several dynamics buttress the glass ceiling effect dynamics of the academy, including subtle bias and racism, the general lack of accountability, and powerful diversity infrastructures designed to create change at the core of institutional culture.

The only way to overcome these dynamics is for leaders to implement a triple-loop organizational learning approach to change that is rooted in an in-depth analysis of the tactics that work, the underlying cultural dynamics that obstruct change, as well as the broader environmental dynamics that enable or constrain change in the academy. Deeply understanding the historical and organizational nature of the problem increases the likelihood of designing policies that will result in lasting change rather than a series of incremental and ineffective stopgap measures. Additionally, establishing a shared vision and common goals is more likely to overcome those factors that contribute to a culture of resistance.

With these objectives in mind, the following set of recommendations are intended to help diversity leaders traverse the three modes of organizational learning: (a) foster a sense of senior leadership support and engagement; (b) develop an appropriate diversity infrastructure to guide change; (c) implement diversity data translation workshops; (d) introduce contextually relevant diversity education programs for search committees, department chairs, faculty, and leaders; (e) establish multiple diversity accountability and incentive systems at the institutional and individual levels; (f) bring research home by translating scholarly research projects into campus-wide conversations that bridge theory and practice; and (g) develop internal mentoring and leadership development programs designed to groom diverse faculty and staff for senior leadership roles on campus.

References

Alger, J. (2009, June). *Diversity in the age of Obama: New directions or status quo? (Employment context)*. Paper presented at the annual meeting of the National Association of College and University Attorneys, Toronto, ON.

Argyris, C., & Schon, D. (1974). *Theory in practice: Increasing professional effectiveness*. San Francisco, CA: Jossey-Bass.

Cox, T., Jr. (2001). *Creating the multicultural organization: A strategy for capturing the power of diversity*. San Francisco, CA: Jossey-Bass.

Dovidio, J. F., Glick, P., & Rudman, L. A. (Eds.). (2005). *Reflecting on the nature of prejudice: Fifty years after Allport*. Malden, MA: Blackwell.

Feldman, M. S. (2004). Resources in emerging structures and processes of change. *Organization Science, 15*(3), 295–309.

Jermier, J. M., Slocum, J. W., Fry, L. W., & Gaines, J. (1991). Organizational subcultures in a soft bureaucracy: Resistance behind the myth and façade of an official culture. *Organization Science, 2*(2), 170–194.

Kezar, A. J. (2000). Higher education at the millennium: Still trees without fruit? *The Review of Higher Education, 23*(4), 443–468.

Milem, J. F., Chang, M. J., & Antonio, A. L. (2005). *Making diversity work on campus: A research-based perspective.* Washington, DC: Association of American Colleges and Universities.

Nealy, M. J. (2008). *ACE: Significant efforts needed to improve diversity in college presidency ranks.* Retrieved from http://diverseeducation.com/article/10619/

Parker, P. S. (2001). African American women executives' leadership communication within dominant-culture organizations: (Re)Conceptualizing notions of collaboration and instrumentality. *Management Communication Quarterly, 15*(1), 42–82.

Paul, M. J. (2003). Double-loop diversity: Applying adult learning theory to the cultivation of diverse learning environments in higher education. *Innovative Higher Education, 28*(1), 35–47.

Piderit, S. K. (2000). Rethinking resistance and recognizing ambivalence: A multidimensional view of attitudes toward an organization change. *The Academy of Management Review, 25*(4), 783–794.

Scharmer, C. O. (2007). *Theory U: Leading from the future as it emerges.* Cambridge, MA: The Society for Organizational Learning.

Schein, E. (2004). *Organizational culture and leadership* (4th ed.). San Francisco, CA: Jossey-Bass.

Senge, P. M. (1990). *The fifth discipline: The art & practice of the learning organization.* New York, NY: Doubleday/Currency.

Senge, P. M., Kleiner, A., Roberts, C., Ross, R., & Smith, B. (1994). *The fifth discipline fieldbook: Strategies and tools for building a learning organization.* New York, NY: Doubleday/Currency.

Smith, D. G., Turner, C. S. V., Osei-Kofi, N., & Richards, S. (2004). Interrupting the usual: Successful strategies for hiring diverse faculty. *The Journal of Higher Education, 75*(2), 133–160.

Williams, D. A. (2013). *Strategic diversity leadership: Activating change and transformation in higher education.* Sterling, VA: Stylus Publishing.

Williams, D. A., Berger, J. B., & McClendon, S. A. (2005). *Toward a model of inclusive excellence and change in postsecondary education.* Washington, DC: Association of American Colleges and Universities.

Williams, D. A., & Wade-Golden, K. C. (2007). *Recorded interview responses from the National Study of Chief Diversity Officers in Higher Education.* Unpublished raw data.

Williams, D. A., & Wade-Golden, K. C. (2008). *The chief diversity officer: A primer for college and university presidents.* Washington, DC: American Council of Education (ACE).

DAMON A. WILLIAMS *is senior vice president, and chief educational and youth development officer at Boys and Girls Clubs of America.*

This chapter serves as a resource for identifying selected programs and initiatives in higher education that demonstrate great promise in addressing glass ceiling effects in the workplace.

Stellar Programs and Initiatives

Raul A. Leon

Addressing glass ceiling effects in the workplace is a significant responsibility and challenge for the field of higher education. It is paramount for educators to familiarize themselves with existing literature concerning the broad range of individual- and institutional-level employment disparities, discuss their effects on position attainment, and engage with programs and initiatives that can remediate these inequalities (Bain & Cummings, 2000; Federal Glass Ceiling Commission, 1995a, 1995b; Jackson & O'Callaghan, 2007; Morley, 2006; Morrison, White, & Van Velsor, 1987).

Previous studies addressing glass ceiling effects have been primarily concerned with those barriers associated with individual-level characteristics, like human capital. This chapter shifts the emphasis to organizations and identifies six programs that challenge institutional dynamics that perpetuate organizational patterns of formal and informal discrimination. These interventions demonstrate great promise in remedying glass ceiling effects. Each program and initiative represents a type of organizational arrangement that can be incorporated into the daily operations of colleges and universities. Table 7.1 presents a brief overview of these six programs and initiatives.

Models for Promoting Institutional Diversity

How can institutions of higher education best address organizational barriers that create a glass ceiling? The first section of this chapter provides a brief overview of the mission, responsibilities, and types of collaboration that define each of the six programs and initiatives. The second section is crafted from a program development perspective in which the researcher offers a compilation of the substantive qualities that characterize these programs and initiatives as successful. While the programs highlighted in this manuscript embody characteristics that can address glass ceiling effects, they are not the only interventions being implemented nationwide

NEW DIRECTIONS FOR INSTITUTIONAL RESEARCH, no. 159 © 2014 Wiley Periodicals, Inc.
Published online in Wiley Online Library (wileyonlinelibrary.com) • DOI: 10.1002/ir.20056

Table 7.1. Stellar Programs Comparison

	Goal	Strategy	Target Population	Collaboration
Recruiting Model	Link the institution and local community	Strong outreach efforts	Local underrepresented job seekers	Local community organizations
Self-Assessment Model	Better institutional knowledge	Conduct self-assessment and self-evaluation	Institutional members	Departments, units, schools, and colleges
Office Model	Guide institutional policy	Collect, analyze, and report faculty data	Faculty	Individuals, offices, and units
Interassociation Model	Discuss issues of leadership	Create a national network of leaders	College and university presidents	Members of professional associations
Institute Model	Promote advancement of women in STEM	Networking and mentoring through workshops and research	Women in science and engineering fields	Student groups, departments, centers, and schools
State Intervention Model	Diversify faculty and staff	Economic support fellowship	Master's and PhD level students	Graduate students, universities, and states

that confront this phenomenon. However, these six offer a comprehensive picture of practices and policies that should not be ignored by institutions of higher education.

Recruiting Model.   Cornell University's Recruitment and Employment Center (REC) serves as a potential resource for job seekers (i.e., faculty and staff) considering Cornell as a place of employment (Cornell University Office of Human Resources, 2007).

Mission.   Cornell's REC mission is twofold: First, it facilitates the work of recruiters and hiring managers to reach qualified applicants; second, it connects candidates with resources and guidance that align with Cornell's broader efforts to diversify its workforce.

Responsibilities and Main Tasks.   Cornell's REC regularly offers employment sessions for prospective staff and faculty from underrepresented groups. The primary role of the REC is to provide employment-seeking individuals with services that range from reviewing employment opportunities to completing the online application processes required for recruiting. The center also connects potential employees with local services such as resume critiquing and practice interview sessions, both of which are invaluable job-hunting resources (Cornell University Office of Human Resources, 2007).

The second main purpose of REC employment sessions is to build formal connections to the university itself through direct guidance. Staff members act as powerful liaisons between applicants and the university, offering a welcoming experience and familiar faces to candidates during the search process (Cornell University Office of Human Resources, 2007). This aspect of the sessions not only makes the job-seeking experience less impersonal but also helps to demonstrate the university's commitment to values beyond their candidates' talents.

One final component of the REC is the Dual Career Program, designed to provide resources like job search assistance to university employment candidates' spouses or partners, particularly for those seeking faculty and staff positions.

Organizational Collaboration.   Cornell's REC operates under the umbrella of the Office of Human Resources. The REC maintains a direct relationship with Cornell's recruiters and hiring managers so that both parties may streamline communication and offer the best opportunities to the best candidates. In an effort to develop further avenues for collaboration, the Cornell Recruitment Partnership (CRP) was also established in 2004, forging a coalition with 38 local organizations to reach and recruit underrepresented candidates including women, people of color, persons with disabilities, veterans, and retirees. Referrals from CRP have contributed to a steady increase in the hiring of diverse candidates, with seven individuals hired in 2004 and a total of 28 new employees in the first nine months of 2006 (Cornell University Office of Human Resources, 2007).

Self-Assessment Model.   The Women's Initiative at Duke is a large-scale research project that launched in 2002 with the objective of better understanding the experiences and challenges that women face at Duke University.

Mission.   Comprehensive in nature, the Women's Initiative at Duke looks beyond the experiences of a single segment of the university community. This initiative explores the lives of faculty, staff, graduate students, undergraduates, and other constituencies representing women affiliated with the university. Its mission is to offer a review of problem areas and distinct opportunities to move toward ensuring more equitable experiences for women across the institution (Duke University Women's Initiative Steering Committee, 2003).

Responsibilities and Main Tasks.   The initiative was borne out of the belief that self-scrutiny and research have the potential to help institutions promote values of inclusiveness and diversity. As such, the Women's Initiative steering committee defined its main task accordingly:

> Formulate questions and methodologies, oversee the gathering and analysis of data by groups of colleagues from every constituency of the university,

and devise policy recommendations based on that data and on our collegial discussions. (Duke University Women's Initiative Steering Committee, 2003, p. 2)

The initiative applied quantitative and qualitative research methods to examine the status of women across the university. This self-study approach provided leaders with rubrics to assess equity and diversity progress, highlighting valuable information to craft plans and strategies that could improve the campus climate for this population. Regarding the status of female faculty at Duke, this initiative gathered data that allowed administrators to compare the representation of women in faculty ranks with respect to their male colleagues. Data were also collected to determine the percentage of female faculty with tenure across departments and the length of time required for women to obtain tenure as compared to their male peers (Duke University Women's Initiative Steering Committee, 2003). The outcomes of this self-study opened the door for conversations about the glass ceiling and encouraged the university to develop appropriate strategies to address existing disparities.

Organizational Collaboration.   Former Duke president Nannerl Keohane served as chair of the Women's Initiative, and 16 individuals representing executive-level positions across campus participated as members of the steering committee. This structure provided the committee with a broad range of perspectives and facilitated the implementation of policy recommendations generated by the official Women's Initiative report (2003). By reporting to the president, the committee achieved an immediate institutional response with the creation of the President's Commission on the Status of Women. This commission was charged with monitoring progress related to the Women's Initiative report's findings. In addition, the provost also created a standing committee on faculty diversity that focuses on search and hiring procedures to secure a diverse pool of applicants.

Office Model.   The Office of Faculty Development and Diversity (FD&D) at Harvard University guides the institutional policy process at the level of faculty affairs with specific attention to faculty recruitment and diversity.

Mission.   FD&D serves as an advocate for women and underrepresented racial and ethnic groups across faculty ranks. This office spearheads a leadership agenda that brings diversity to the forefront of campus activity and seeks to improve the work-life conditions for all faculty members (Harvard University Office of the Vice Provost, 2008).

Responsibilities and Main Tasks.   FD&D collects, analyzes, and reports on data intended to review and monitor faculty appointments. The office has become a central resource center for demographic data collection relevant to faculty promotion. One of the main responsibilities of FD&D is to implement university-wide programs that support the recommendations of the 2005 Women's Task Force. The office also assists units across campus in implementing and evaluating a myriad of diversity initiatives. This support comes in the form of office staff assigned to work with groups across campus, technical assistance, financial start-up capital, leadership, and guidance in advancing new policies and initiatives (President and Fellows of Harvard College, 2009).

All these strategies and rigorous data collection processes have been summarized in reports produced by FD&D (Harvard University Office of the Vice Provost, 2008; President and Fellows of Harvard College, 2009). This commitment to documentation aligns with the university's goal to foster intellectual leadership within its own ranks and to "share ideas and strategies to tackle the challenges of recruiting, developing, promoting, and retaining the best scholars in the world" (Harvard University Office of the Vice Provost, 2008, p. 66).

Organizational Collaboration. FD&D is the central administration's faculty affairs office, operating from the Office of the Senior Vice Provost. To enforce accountability, FD&D reports annually on the equity and diversity progress made throughout the institution, collecting reports from Harvard's 12 schools to assess their progress and document any challenges in advancing the university's diversity agenda. Because Harvard University is a highly decentralized organization, FD&D partners with multiple units and departments across campus to develop a common culture that prioritizes faculty development and diversity.

Illustrating the collaborative nature of this work, FD&D has partnered with the Office of Institutional Research to establish an institutional baseline to target recruitment and retention of faculty of color. In addition, FD&D has also piloted numerous programs and initiatives at the institutional level that involve faculty across all ranks. For instance, FD&D has been instrumental in funding postdoctoral fellows and junior faculty members, yet it has also addressed issues such as high-quality child care and has assisted scholars in finding balance between their family and career lives (Harvard University Office of the Vice Provost, 2008).

Interassociation Model. The American Council on Education's (ACE) Spectrum Initiative is a multiyear national agenda that seeks to diversify the pool of candidates aspiring to the position of college presidency.

Mission. Data indicate that 42% of college presidents in 1986 were 50 years old or younger and just 14% were 61 or older. Some 20 years later, only 8% were 50 or younger and 49% were 61 or older (Renick, 2008). This age-related phenomenon presents an opportunity for institutions to broaden their pool of applicants and foster more inclusive search processes to diversify the ranks of college presidents. The Spectrum Initiative was launched to assist current leaders from underrepresented backgrounds who aspire to reach executive positions, reframing the model utilized by search and screen committees when selecting candidates.

Responsibilities and Main Tasks. The Spectrum Initiative is a multiyear national agenda designed to diversify executive-level positions in higher education. This initiative is sponsored by the Center for Advancement of Racial and Ethnic Equity (CAREE) at ACE and is guided by three specific objectives: (a) to broaden and strengthen the leadership pipeline for women and racial/ethnic minority administrators; (b) to ensure that presidential search and selection processes are inclusive; and (c) to promote leadership development, mentoring, and succession planning (American Council on Education, 2008).

Organizational Collaboration.   The Spectrum Initiative is the result of collaboration among a group of leading higher education associations that convened in March 2007. ACE firmly believes that research is a critical step in identifying suitable women and minority candidates who aspire to the college presidency. Relying on a strong relationship with institutional boards of trustees, national and regional associations, executive search firms, and campus search communities, ACE has secured access to demographic information that identifies individuals working in administrative positions that have a high likelihood of leading to the presidency (Renick, 2008).

Using this information, ACE designs programs that prepare aspiring candidates from underrepresented backgrounds to assume executive-level roles such as the college presidency (Renick, 2008). ACE has sponsored roundtables that explore the best practices for governing boards, organized peer mentoring networks, and developed presidential candidate database and referral systems to support these candidates. Among these sponsored programs, a summit for women of color administrators in higher education has been instrumental in establishing mentoring relationships and facilitating interactions between aspiring candidates, current and former women presidents, and chancellors of color (American Council on Education, 2008).

Institute Model.   The Women in Science & Engineering Leadership Institute (WISELI) is a research center at the University of Wisconsin-Madison that seeks to address impediments to the academic advancement of women scientists and engineers.

Mission.   WISELI's website affirms that its guiding mission is to foster a research agenda, networking opportunities, and a mentoring structure that define WISELI as a "living laboratory" where issues relevant to women in science and engineering are carefully examined. The organization's long-term goal is to increase the percentage of female faculty and leadership positions in higher education to 50%, a figure roughly equivalent to the representation of women in the university's student body (Women in Science & Engineering Leadership Institute, 2013).

Responsibilities and Main Tasks.   WISELI is devoted to the creation of formal and informal networking venues for faculty and postdoctoral fellows in otherwise predominantly male environments. WISELI provides a space for faculty to explore issues ranging from pipeline discussions for women aspiring to careers in the sciences, to development workshops for scholars facing issues involving child care or parental leave. WISELI's main task is to reduce isolation, build relationships, and foster an environment that welcomes women in science and engineering fields (Women in Science & Engineering Leadership Institute, 2013).

Organizational Collaboration.   WISELI is funded through a combination of several administrative partners that include eight different units within University of Wisconsin-Madison, grants from national scientific funding agencies, and gifts or income-generating activities sponsored by WISELI itself. WISELI engages individuals at different levels of their profession, women who represent several schools, departments, and units across campus that retain connections to science and engineering fields. WISELI offers grants and monetary support to implement programs across the institution, sponsors workshops and forums, and continues to build partnerships that promote the participation and advancement of women in science and engineering.

State Intervention Model.   The Diversifying Higher Education Faculty in Illinois Program (DFI) is a fellowship initiative administered by the Illinois Board of Higher Education (IBHE). DFI provides annual financial assistance to over 100 members of traditionally underrepresented groups to pursue graduate and professional degrees in institutions of higher education in Illinois (Illinois Board of Higher Education, 2011).

Mission.   DFI was designed to increase the number of traditionally underrepresented individuals in faculty, staff, and governing board positions. DFI currently combines the Illinois Consortium for Educational Opportunity Program (ICEOP) and the Illinois Minority Graduate Incentive Program (IMGIP) into a single fellowship.

Responsibilities and Main Tasks.   One of the main responsibilities of DFI representatives is to identify and contact qualified candidates with demonstrated financial need. All academic fields are considered for this award. The DFI Board approved an allocation of $1.64 million for the fiscal year 2012 to fund 130 fellowship awards (Illinois Board of Higher Education, 2011).

Organizational Collaboration.   DFI was established by the Illinois General Assembly in 2004. The DFI Act authorizes the Illinois Board of Higher Education (IBHE) to appoint a 21-member board to establish policies and procedures to administer the DFI program. Each participating college or university is accountable to the IBHE, with DFI representatives acting as the main link between candidates and the state of Illinois. Starting with the application process, candidates must submit materials to their institution's DFI program representative. Each institution then determines which applications are sent forward to the statewide selections committee. In the second phase, a state selection committee of DFI board members reviews the applications and grants the fellowship awards (Illinois Board of Higher Education, 2011).

Upon graduation, students receiving fellowships must agree to seek and accept a teaching or staff full-time appointment in an Illinois postsecondary educational institution or governing board. If this career path is not pursued, students must accept administrative or education-related positions as employees of the state of Illinois equal to the number of years of DFI fellowship support (Illinois Board of Higher Education, 2011).

Discussion

This chapter outlined six programs and initiatives that confront the glass ceiling and offer varying levels of support toward the advancement of women and underrepresented populations in higher education. No single program or initiative described is fully capable of remediating or eliminating the effects of the glass ceiling on its own. Yet, examining these six models provides an opportunity to analyze several strategies in action, allowing for a discussion that considers higher education workforce dynamics beyond the context of any single institution.

These programs and initiatives were selected because they devote resources to creating work environments that recognize and value diversity as an organizational asset. As such, characteristics from each of the six models could be adopted and replicated to enhance the experience of women and people of color in the higher education workforce. This section highlights six simple but compelling principles distilled from each of the aforementioned six programs.

Recruiting Locally. The recruiting model exemplifies the benefits available for institutions that reach into their communities and provide individuals with the opportunity to learn about the institution as a future place of employment. By securing partnerships with local organizations, the recruiting model demonstrates that institutions must find new ways to reach talented individuals. In this case, these partnerships streamline the process of identifying and hiring candidates from underrepresented groups. The recruiting model makes the hiring process less impersonal, communicating the institution's concern with candidates' professional future, and thereby encouraging underrepresented candidates to consider careers there.

To ensure that institutions have a diverse pool of applicants, they must build connections to local organizations, strengthen links with professional associations, and continue to establish positive relationships with the local community. It is also beneficial to observe and learn from those institutions that have currently demonstrated success in recruiting a diverse workforce. When setting priorities, institutions cannot ignore their ties with other campuses across the nation as well as their local community. As more institutions focus on preparing graduates to contribute not only nationally, but also at the state and local levels, it is essential for universities to do the same, connecting individuals from the local community with the university as a potential place of employment for a successful career.

Self-Assessment and Self-Evaluation. The self-assessment model teaches a valuable lesson that in order to develop a work environment that

NEW DIRECTIONS FOR INSTITUTIONAL RESEARCH • DOI: 10.1002/ir

overcomes glass ceiling barriers, institutions must know where they currently stand on issues of diversity. This model is rooted in the concept of self-scrutiny and highlights the importance of feedback from diverse constituencies. To understand the hidden nature of glass ceiling barriers, this model relies on reporting structures that enhance accountability, guide institutional policy, and offer a realistic view of current challenges and opportunities.

Understanding the current status of women and people of color in the workforce nationally is a priority that can no longer be ignored. In higher education, despite recent gains in the area of diversity, many institutions still struggle to create environments that are inclusive for all populations. When institutions devote time to better understanding the experiences and challenges of a group in their organization, they position themselves to discover valuable information in assessing their own progress toward demonstrating their values and priorities. This first step is critical in building the foundation for a campus that integrates diversity as an institutional asset.

The Importance of Data.   The office model is presented as a prototype of a well-articulated collaborative leadership approach. This model involves building relationships of mutual responsibility and collaboration, shattering institutional silos, and in turn fostering greater faculty diversity. The office model shows that leadership support must extend beyond promises for change, where devoting staff, financial support, technical assistance, and guiding departments and units is a commitment that must be present from start to finish.

In this model, collecting and analyzing data is as important as leaders who are innovative and can motivate departments and units to consider the implications of these data in their daily work. Data can provide a better baseline for the implementation of a myriad of initiatives across campus. However, it is critical to possess staff and resources that can facilitate these departments' and units' efforts to envision how their work may align with broader diversity priorities. Often, the work of managing and running programs day to day can be all-consuming. A dedicated staff focused on enhancing diversity can be an effective collaborator, advocating for diversity as part of what an organization does on a daily basis, avoiding organizational misalignment and maximizing resources.

Connecting Beyond Institutional Boundaries.   The major strength of the interassociation model is its potential to connect individuals and institutions across national networks. In particular, the model offers a space for participants to discuss topics and trends that affect the future of leadership roles in higher education. The success of this model relies upon the ability of its participants to bring ideas back to their own campuses, extending the conversation, and creating venues to implement plans and strategies.

Formal mentoring and networking programs help improve connectivity within organizations. When these programs are replicated at the regional and national scale, they ensure that individuals are introduced to a wide array of ideas and connect with others in leadership positions across the nation. A fundamental benefit of this practice is that individuals can interact with experienced leaders in spaces designed for innovative thinking that extend beyond institutional borders.

Institutional Mentoring, Networking, and Developing Opportunities.   The institute model creates support systems based on mentoring structures and networking opportunities that allow participants to pursue their academic interests. At its core, the institute model stands out because it connects women in science and engineering fields at different stages in their careers. Additionally, this model positions research at the center of the academic community, creating a supportive environment aligned with the career aspirations of these professionals.

Mentoring and networking are practices widely recognized as crucial to professional development in organizations. The institute model incorporates these practices in a collaborative research oriented environment. When organizations invest resources in designing programs and initiatives that are this comprehensive in nature, they can fulfill multiple goals, such as demonstrating their commitment to employees by creating environments that reduce professional isolation while also encouraging collaborative work across department and units.

Financial Commitment and Support.   The state intervention model stresses the importance of identifying and supporting future academic and administrative leaders in the early stages of their education. This program prioritizes the recruitment of underrepresented groups with fellowships that provide powerful economic incentives to pursue careers in higher education. The state intervention model stands out because fellowship recipients are required to seek and apply for jobs in higher education and must do so in the same state. Therefore, this model ensures that investments in candidates will eventually benefit colleges and universities across the state.

When organizations make commitments to diversity, experienced people are needed to translate these commitments into action, to gather resources to implement programs and initiatives with a keen understanding of the challenges that prevent diversity from being championed as an institutional priority. In the context of economic challenges, many colleges and universities face budget constraints that can impede this work. Therefore, institutions must recognize that investing in diversity, when properly managed, can bring sizeable individual and institutional benefits— a principle that must be repeatedly emphasized with respect to the glass ceiling.

Conclusion

The six programs and initiatives detailed in this chapter represent varying approaches that can be replicated and adapted to reduce or even eradicate the glass ceiling in higher education. The potential impact of these organizational responses targeting the glass ceiling from different dimensions, when considered collectively, constitutes a remarkably wide-ranging effort. The presence of faculty, administrators, and staff who are truly representative of our diverse society ultimately stands to benefit all of higher education.

Each program signifies an organization that has chosen to proactively support an environment that confronts glass ceiling effects. These initiatives are a reminder that our institutions can no longer stand still and hope increasing numbers of women and minorities will automatically reach leadership positions. Organizations must be involved, proactive, engaged, willing to devote resources and reconsider misconceptions, and above all, answer to new waves of diverse talent knocking on their doors.

References

American Council on Education. (2008). The Spectrum initiative: Advancing diversity in the college presidency. *The Presidency*, Winter (Suppl.). Retrieved from http://www.acenet.edu/about-ace/special-initiatives/Pages/The-Spectrum-Initiative.aspx

Bain, O., & Cummings, W. (2000). Academe's glass ceiling: Societal, professional/organizational, and institutional barriers to the career advancement of academic women. *Comparative Education Review*, *44*(4), 493–514.

Cornell University Office of Human Resources. (2007). Cornell recruitment efforts involve community outreach. *WorkLife Digest*. Retrieved from https://www.hr.cornell.edu/diversity/recruitment/recruitment_partnership.html

Duke University Women's Initiative Steering Committee. (2003). *Women's initiative*. Retrieved from http://universitywomen.stanford.edu/reports/WomensInitiativeReport.pdf

Federal Glass Ceiling Commission. (1995a). *A solid investment: Making full use of the nation's human capital*. Washington, DC: U.S. Department of Labor.

Federal Glass Ceiling Commission. (1995b). *Good for business: Making full use of the nation's human capital*. Washington, DC: U.S. Department of Labor.

Harvard University Office of the Vice Provost. (2008). *Faculty development & diversity: End of year report*. Retrieved from http://www.faculty.harvard.edu/sites/default/files/downloads/FD%26D%20End%20of%20Year%20Report%202008%20-%20Full%20Report.pdf

Illinois Board of Higher Education. (2011). *Diversifying faculty in Illinois Program Fiscal Year 2012 Grant Allocation*. Retrieved from http://www.ibhe.state.il.us/Board/agendas/2011/August/ItemD-14.pdf

Jackson, J. F. L., & O'Callaghan, E. M. (2007). *The glass ceiling: A misunderstood form of discrimination, an annotated bibliography*. Milwaukee: Institute on Race and Ethnicity, University of Wisconsin System.

Morley, L. (2006). Hidden transcripts: The micropolitics of gender in commonwealth universities. *Women's Studies International Forum*, *29*(6), 543–551.

Morrison, A. M., White, R. P., & Van Velsor, E. (1987). *Breaking the glass ceiling: Can women reach the top of America's largest corporations?* Reading, MA: Addison-Wesley.

President and Fellows of Harvard College. (2009). *Faculty Development and Diversity Annual Reports*. Retrieved from http://www.faculty.harvard.edu/about-office/fdd-annual-reports

NEW DIRECTIONS FOR INSTITUTIONAL RESEARCH • DOI: 10.1002/ir

Renick, J. (2008, Winter). The Spectrum initiative: Advancing diversity in the college presidency. *The Presidency*, *11*, 1–8.
Women in Science & Engineering Leadership Institute (WISELI). (2013). *"Learn about WISELI," The Board of Regents of the University of Wisconsin System*. Retrieved from http://wiseli.engr.wisc.edu/about.php

RAUL A. LEON *is an assistant professor of higher education at Eastern Michigan University.*

INDEX

Powell, G. N., 3, 37–38
Programs and initiatives, addressing glass ceiling effects, 85–95; comparison of, 86; institute model, 90–91, 94; interassociation model, 89–90, 93–94; office model, 88–89, 93; overview, 85; recruiting model, 86–87, 92; self-assessment model, 87–88, 92–93; state intervention model, 91–92, 94
PSID. *See* Panel Study of Income Dynamics (PSID)

Qualitative research, on glass ceiling, 28–30, 33–34

Ragins, B. R., 37
Renick, J., 89–90
Reskin, B., 3, 39
Richards, S., 57, 76
Ridgeway, C. L., 3, 39
Rindfleisch, A., 41
Ritchey, P. N., 17
Roberts, C., 81
Robinson, G., 3
Ross, R., 81
Rosser, S. V., 39
Rosser, V. J., 13, 19, 23
Ross-Smith, A., 39
Rudman, L. A., 78–79
Ryan, A. M., 14–15
Ryu, M., 6, 50

Sadao, K. C., 20
Sagaria, M. M., 4, 8
Salary-equity policies, 19–21
Salary-equity studies, 14–19; data analysis techniques in, selection of, 16–18; findings of, 18–19; hierarchical linear modeling in, 16, 17; individual growth modeling in, 17; Ordinary Least Squares in, 16–17; sample selection in, 14; variable selection in, 14–16
Sallee, M. W., 49
Scharmer, C. O., 80
Schein, E., 76
Schellhardt, T., 2
Schmidt, A., 27
Schon, D., 76
Scott, J. A., 17

Semyonov, M., 17
Senge, P. M., 76, 80–81
Sequeira, J. M., 38
Shea, J. A., 39
Sikora, A. C., 5
Slocum, J. W., 77
Smith, B., 81
Smith, D. G., 57, 76
Smolinski, C., 64, 66
Snyder, J. K., 14
Snyder, T. D., 51
Solórzano, D. G., 31
Stefancic, J., 31
Stern, D. T., 39
Stevens, D. D., 49, 57, 59
Stewman, S., 38
Stockdale, M., 39
Strayhorn, T. L., 64
Stutz, J., 64, 68, 71
Sullivan, J., 14–15
Survey of Earned Doctorates (SED), 16

Tate, W. F., IV, 31
Thomas, D., 2
Thompson, D. E., 37
Thorsteinson, T., 14–15
Tierney, W. G., 49, 53
Toutkoushian, R. K., 14–15, 17–20
Townsend, B., 37
Trice, A. G., 49, 56
Trower, C. A., 5, 51, 67
Turner, C. S. V., 4, 8, 20, 53, 57, 76

Umbach, P. D., 15–17

Valdes, F., 31
Van den Brink, M., 39
Vanderlinden, K. E., 49
Vanneman, R., 3–4, 8, 13, 20, 26–28, 37–39, 44, 65
Van Velsor, E., 3, 85
Von Glinow, M. A., 2–3, 38–39, 64
Von Velsor, E., 37–39

Wade-Golden, K. C., 76, 78, 79
Wall Street Journal, 2
Webster, J., 26–27
Weick, K. E., 52, 54–55
Werner, S., 39
White, R. P., 3, 37–39, 85

OTHER TITLES AVAILABLE IN THE
NEW DIRECTIONS FOR INSTITUTIONAL RESEARCH SERIES
John F. Ryan, Editor-in-Chief
Gloria Crisp, Associate Editor

government needs, economic restructuring, information technology, and student and staff mobility. Institutional researchers have a critical role to play in addressing these issues. In this volume, we have embedded the practice of IR as experienced globally. We brought together a discussion that is delivered from multiple perspectives, but fundamentally one that draws from the collaborative efforts of practitioners across borders. By embedding notions of globalization that affect IR, we can engage readers in broad discussions on where we are coming from and where we are heading.
ISBN: 978-1-1187-1435-5

IR 156   **Benchmarking in Institutional Research**
Gary D. Levy, Nicolas A. Valcik
The term *benchmarking* is commonplace nowadays in institutional research and higher education. Less common, however, is a general understanding of what it really means and how it has been, and can be, used effectively. This volume of *New Directions for Institutional Research* begins by defining benchmarking as "a strategic and structured approach whereby an organization compares aspects of its processes and/or outcomes to those of another organization or set of organizations to identify opportunities for improvement."

Building on this definition, the chapters in this volume provide a brief history of the evolution and emergence of benchmarking in general and in higher education in particular. The authors apply benchmarking to enrollment management and student success, institutional effectiveness, and the potential economic impact of higher education institutions on their host communities. They look at the use of national external survey data in institutional benchmarking and selection of peer institutions, introduce multivariate statistical methodologies for guiding that selection, and consider a novel application of baseball sabermetric methods. The volume offers a solid starting point for those new to benchmarking in higher education and provides examples of current best practices and prospective new directions.
ISBN: 978-1-1186-0883-8

IR 155   **Refining the Focus on Faculty Diversity in Postsecondary Institutions**
Yonghong Jade Xu
Faculty diversity is gaining unprecedented emphasis in the mission of colleges and universities, and institutional researchers are being pushed for relevant data. In this volume, six chapters examine faculty diversity from a variety of perspectives. Together, they constitute a comprehensive outlook on the subject, highlighting factors including racial background, gender, citizenship, employment status, and academic discipline, and examining how growing diversity has affected the work experience and productivity of faculty and the learning outcomes of students. Special attention is given to international and nontenure-track faculty members, two groups that have experienced rapid growth in recent years. Chapter authors present empirical evidence to support the increasing importance of faculty diversity in institutional research, to show the need for actively tracking the changes in diversity over time, and to highlight the critical role of research methodology in all such work.
ISBN: 978-1-1185-2675-0

IR 154   **Multilevel Modeling Techniques and Applications in Institutional
          Research**
          Joe L. Lott, II, and James S. Antony
          Multilevel modeling is an increasingly popular multivariate technique that is
          widely applied in the social sciences. Increasingly, institutional research (IR)
          practitioners are making instructional decisions based on results from their
          multivariate analyses, which often come from nested data that lend
          themselves to multilevel modeling techniques. As colleges and universities
          continue to face mounting pressures to shrink their budgets and maximize
          resources while at the same time maintaining and even increasing their
          institutional profiles, data-driven decision making will be critical. Multilevel
          modeling is one tool that will lead to more efficient estimates and enhance
          understanding of complex relationships.
              The express purpose of this volume of *New Directions for Institutional
          Research* is to illustrate both the theoretical underpinnings and practical
          applications of multilevel modeling in IR. Chapters in this volume introduce
          the fundamental concepts of multilevel modeling techniques in both a
          conceptual and technical manner. Authors provide a range of examples of
          nested models that are based on linear and categorical outcomes, and then
          offer important suggestions about presenting results of multilevel models
          through charts and graphs.
          ISBN: 978-1-1184-4400-9

IR 153   **Data Use in the Community College**
          Christopher M. Mullin, Trudy Bers, and Linda Serra Hagedorn
          American community colleges represent a true success story. With their
          multiple missions, they have provided access and opportunity to millions of
          students who would not have otherwise had the opportunity to gain a college
          degree, certificate, or technical training. But community colleges are held
          accountable for their services and must be able to show that they are indeed
          serving their variety of students appropriately. Providing that evidence is the
          responsibility of the institutional research office, which must function not
          only as the data collection point but also as the decipherer of the story the
          different types of data tell.
              This volume speaks of the multiplicity of data required to tell the
          community college story. The authors explore and detail how various
          sources—workforce data, market data, state-level data, federal data, and, of
          course, institutional data such as transcript files—all have something to say
          about the life of a community college. Much like an orchestral score, where
          the different parts played by individual instruments become music under the
          hands of a conductor, these data can be coordinated and assembled into a
          message that answers questions of student success and institutional
          effectiveness.
          ISBN: 978-1-1183-8807-5

NEW DIRECTIONS FOR INSTITUTIONAL RESEARCH
ORDER FORM SUBSCRIPTION AND SINGLE ISSUES

DISCOUNTED BACK ISSUES:

Use this form to receive 20% off all back issues of *New Directions for Institutional Research*.
All single issues priced at **$23.20** (normally $29.00)

TITLE	ISSUE NO.	ISBN
_____	_____	_____
_____	_____	_____
_____	_____	_____

Call 888-378-2537 or see mailing instructions below. When calling, mention the promotional code JBNND to receive your discount. For a complete list of issues, please visit www.josseybass.com/go/ndir

SUBSCRIPTIONS: (1 YEAR, 4 ISSUES)

☐ New Order   ☐ Renewal

U.S.	☐ Individual: $89	☐ Institutional: $317
CANADA/MEXICO	☐ Individual: $89	☐ Institutional: $357
ALL OTHERS	☐ Individual: $113	☐ Institutional: $391

Call 888-378-2537 or see mailing and pricing instructions below.
Online subscriptions are available at www.onlinelibrary.wiley.com

ORDER TOTALS:

Issue / Subscription Amount: $ _____

Shipping Amount: $ _____
(for single issues only – subscription prices include shipping)

Total Amount: $ _____

SHIPPING CHARGES:

First Item $6.00
Each Add'l Item $2.00

(No sales tax for U.S. subscriptions. Canadian residents, add GST for subscription orders. Individual rate subscriptions must be paid by personal check or credit card. Individual rate subscriptions may not be resold as library copies.)

BILLING & SHIPPING INFORMATION:

☐ **PAYMENT ENCLOSED:** *(U.S. check or money order only. All payments must be in U.S. dollars.)*

☐ **CREDIT CARD:** ☐ VISA ☐ MC ☐ AMEX

Card number _____ Exp. Date _____

Card Holder Name _____ Card Issue # _____

Signature _____ Day Phone _____

☐ **BILL ME:** *(U.S. institutional orders only. Purchase order required.)*

Purchase order # _____
Federal Tax ID 13559302 • GST 89102-8052

Name _____

Address _____

Phone _____ E-mail _____

Copy or detach page and send to: **John Wiley & Sons, One Montgomery Street, Suite 1200, San Francisco, CA 94104-4594**

Order Form can also be faxed to: **888-481-2665**

PROMO JBNND